PAUL SALAZAR

AI Agents Explained

The Next Frontier of Intelligence

First published by Artificial Intelligence Press 2025

First edition

This book was professionally typeset on Reedsy.
Find out more at reedsy.com

Contents

PAUL SALAZAR

AI Agents Explained

The Next Frontier of Intelligence

First published by Artificial Intelligence Press 2025

First edition

This book was professionally typeset on Reedsy.
Find out more at reedsy.com

1

The Dawn of AI Agents

In our ever-evolving digital era, artificial intelligence (AI) has swiftly become one of the most talked-about and transformative fields. From suggested playlists on music streaming platforms to algorithms that process our photos to our virtual assistants answering queries on the go, AI has quietly—and not so quietly—entered our daily lives. Yet, behind these flashy demonstrations of cutting-edge technology lies an even more profound development: the rise of AI agents. These are systems designed not only to perform tasks but to do so autonomously, adapting to new circumstances, learning from their experiences, and working collaboratively when necessary. This chapter will introduce these remarkable AI agents, explain what makes them stand apart from other forms of AI, and illustrate why they hold so much promise (and risk) in reshaping our world.

A New Kind of Intelligence

The term "AI agents" may sound intimidating to a newcomer, conjuring up images of either hyperintelligent robots or the cold, futuristic visions of science fiction. Yet, an agent is simply an entity that can perceive its environment, make decisions based on those perceptions, and act in pursuit of a goal. When combined with artificial intelligence, these agents can learn from the actions they take and the outcomes they produce, effectively becoming more sophisticated and capable over time.

To understand why AI agents are unique, consider the difference between a typical "dumb" computer program and something that is "agentic." A traditional program might follow a fixed set of instructions: if you click a button, it opens a file; if you select a different option, it processes some data. It does these tasks reliably, but it doesn't learn or adapt. In contrast, an AI agent has the capacity to change its behavior if it notices that certain patterns in the environment require a different strategy. Instead of being locked into a narrow procedure, it can make judgment calls and even develop new tactics that its human programmers didn't explicitly code. This leap from static programming to adaptive behavior is the core of what makes AI agents so powerful.

From Simple Beginnings to Sophisticated Autonomy

Although AI agents may seem like a contemporary phenomenon, their conceptual roots go back decades. Early forms of AI were primarily symbolic: researchers designed programs that used human-created rules and logic structures to solve specific problems. These "expert systems" did provide glimpses into the potential of AI, especially in specialized fields such as medical diagnosis or resource allocation, but they were limited. They lacked the ability to learn from experience and adapt to new scenarios without extensive reprogramming.

Over time, breakthroughs in machine learning—especially deep learning—opened doors to a new wave of AI applications. Machine learning enabled systems to derive patterns from large datasets and then use those learned patterns to make predictions or decisions. Yet even then, a typical machine learning system might only serve a single, well-defined purpose: classify images, transcribe speech, or predict the next word in a sentence. An AI agent, on the other hand, combines these learning capabilities with an awareness of its environment and the ability to proactively decide what action to take next.

For instance, consider a self-driving car. It is essentially an AI agent trained to navigate roads safely. It "sees" (through sensors like cameras and radar) and interprets the environment (lane markings, traffic signals, pedestrians). It then decides on a course of action (accelerate, brake, turn) and continuously refines its decision-making based on feedback (did the car maintain a safe distance?). This ongoing loop of perception, decision, and action makes the vehicle agentic, because it can handle a variety of real-world scenarios—driving on city streets, highways, in different weather conditions—and adapt its behavior accordingly.

Agents in Everyday Life

While self-driving cars provide a dramatic example, not all AI agents are this large-scale or visible. Indeed, many agents operate quietly in the background, enhancing software and services we use every day. Chatbots on customer service websites are often powered by AI agents that can infer the user's intent and direct them to relevant solutions or escalate the conversation to a human agent if the interaction becomes too complex. Recommendation systems on e-commerce platforms can be considered agents that track your browsing and purchasing behavior, adapt to your evolving tastes, and suggest products you might like.

Increasingly, we see AI-driven personal assistants—like Siri, Google Assistant, and Alexa—taking on more agent-like qualities. Rather than just responding to direct commands ("Play music," "What's the weather?"), they are slowly learning from our habits, offering reminders, scheduling tasks, or even making recommendations before we've explicitly requested them. As these assistants grow in sophistication and integrate with more services (from our calendars to our thermostats), they begin to resemble a genuine AI agent that can orchestrate multiple tasks and adapt its suggestions to our personal preferences.

These "daily life" examples highlight how AI agents are already woven into the fabric of modern living. Yet for many people, the technology works like magic: they see the outcome (recommendations, driving directions, voice interactions) without necessarily understanding how. This opacity can be both fascinating and unsettling. On the one hand, it's convenient to simply trust the agent to handle tasks without manual oversight. On the other, it raises legitimate questions about privacy, accountability, and whether we're giving up too much control to systems we barely grasp.

Why AI Agents Matter

AI agents hold the potential to revolutionize industries and change the way society functions on multiple levels. For instance, in healthcare, an intelligent diagnostic agent could parse through medical records, genomic data, and real-time patient information to suggest personalized treatment plans—guiding doctors with insights that even the best-trained human might overlook. In finance, autonomous trading agents can execute complex strategies in fractions of a second, though their speed and sophistication also introduce new forms of market volatility and risk. In logistics and manufacturing, fleets of AI-powered robots and drones might coordinate to optimize supply chains, reducing waste and cost, while potentially displacing certain types of human labor.

Beyond the commercial sphere, AI agents could help tackle global problems. Climate modeling agents, for example, might analyze huge volumes of data and simulate various policy scenarios to provide early warning for environmental crises. Disaster response agents might coordinate rescue robots, ensuring relief supplies get to where they're needed most quickly and efficiently. Educational agents could personalize learning pathways for students around the world, scaling high-quality instruction to places and populations that currently lack resources.

All of these possibilities hinge on the fact that AI agents bring a level of autonomy and adaptiveness that conventional software struggles to match. By constantly learning and refining their behavior, agents can operate in messy, ever-changing environments—precisely the kinds of complex scenarios that make up real-world challenges. This is the core reason why AI agents matter and why they generate so much excitement and optimism.

Balancing Promise and Peril

Of course, no technological leap is entirely free of controversy or risks. As AI agents gain more independence, questions arise about ethics, transparency, and accountability. How do we prevent algorithms from inheriting harmful biases that exist in their training data, resulting in unfair or prejudiced outcomes? If an AI-driven agent in a self-driving car makes a split-second decision that results in a crash, who is held liable? And as agents become more capable, will entire categories of jobs become obsolete, leaving workers underprepared for an automated future?

These ethical and social challenges are not trivial. In fact, they sit at the heart of debates among technologists, policymakers, and ethicists. Because AI agents are designed to adapt and optimize, their decision-making processes can become opaque, even to their creators. This phenomenon, often referred to as the "black box problem," underscores the difficulty in explaining exactly *why* an agent chose a particular action. In some cases, a lack of transparency can lead to mistrust or misuse, so there is a growing push for "explainable AI" frameworks to help users and regulators understand how AI agents arrive at their conclusions.

At the societal level, we must also consider how to distribute the benefits of AI agents equitably. If these technologies remain in the hands of a privileged few—well-funded corporations or wealthy nations—the global imbalance could deepen existing inequalities. On the other hand, if we invest in education, open-source projects, and collaborative research, AI agents might become a universal tool for problem-solving and innovation. These are open questions that will shape how AI evolves in the coming decades.

Making AI Agents Accessible

For the average person, "AI agents" can seem like an abstract concept with little direct relevance to their day-to-day routine. Yet in truth, these agents have already started working behind the scenes—often improving efficiency or providing conveniences that we take for granted. From automated customer support to smarter navigation apps, the early stages of agent-based technology are pervasive. As they continue to evolve, it's helpful to have at least a basic understanding of what an AI agent is, how it learns, and why it might make certain decisions in certain contexts.

Perhaps one of the most accessible entry points to understanding AI agents is through personal experimentation. Numerous online platforms now provide simple, intuitive interfaces for experimenting with machine learning models—many of which can be turned into basic agent-like programs. Whether it's playing a training game that uses reinforcement learning or tinkering with a chatbot that uses a large language model, these hands-on experiences can demystify the concept. When people recognize that these systems operate through trial-and-error learning, pattern detection, and a feedback loop, AI agents become less of a sci-fi plot device and more of a tangible technology that anyone can explore.

A Brief Look Ahead

As the capabilities of AI agents advance, we stand on the cusp of an era in which these intelligent tools may handle everything from mundane household chores (like vacuuming or ordering groceries) to critical responsibilities (like monitoring national power grids or aiding in complex surgeries). In subsequent chapters, we will explore these possibilities in greater depth—looking at how AI agents evolved from simple rule-followers to advanced learning systems, how they're applied in various industries, and how we can harness their power responsibly and ethically.

Understanding *why* AI agents represent such a big leap in technology is crucial. Conventional software follows predetermined rules, whereas AI agents can rewrite their own strategies based on new information. This grants them a remarkable kind of flexibility—one that can be harnessed for enormous benefit but also necessitates caution, oversight, and thoughtful design. Readers should keep this duality in mind: the very features that make AI agents so promising are also the ones that make them potentially disruptive. Managing that tension will be a central challenge as we continue to integrate intelligent agents into the core of our societies.

A Wider View

"The Dawn of AI Agents" is not just about celebrating a technical breakthrough. It's about recognizing that technology is never developed or deployed in a vacuum. Social, economic, and cultural factors all intertwine with the adoption of AI agents. What these systems become will depend on the collective decisions made by researchers, corporations, governments, and everyday users. Indeed, the trajectory of AI agents is still being written, and understanding the fundamentals will help shape a future that maximizes their benefits while mitigating their risks.

In this light, the broader goal of this book is to invite you to take a meaningful step beyond the headlines and marketing hype. By examining the history, mechanics, applications, and consequences of AI agents, we can better grasp the magnitude of this transformation. We will look at the technical elements that allow these systems to function, scrutinize the real-world deployments that are already changing the way we live and work, and wrestle with the ethical dilemmas that arise from giving decision-making power to non-human entities. The chapters ahead aim to equip you, the reader, with the knowledge and perspective needed to navigate an increasingly agent-driven world.

Conclusion

The dawn of AI agents is upon us. While it's easy to overlook their presence—since we may not interact with them consciously every single day—their influence is expanding rapidly. By learning from data, adapting to real-world feedback, and functioning autonomously, AI agents represent a new milestone in the journey of artificial intelligence. They challenge our assumptions about what machines can do, and they demand that we consider both the extraordinary benefits and the legitimate concerns that accompany such transformative technology.

As we progress through the rest of this book, we will revisit key themes introduced in this chapter: how AI agents differ from traditional software, how they learn and make decisions, and how they are already revolutionizing industries from healthcare to transportation. We'll also delve deeper into the ethical, legal, and societal implications that arise when we begin to trust autonomous agents with increasing levels of responsibility. By the end, it should be clear why AI agents have the potential to reshape not only our workplaces and economies but also our collective imagination about what it means to be intelligent, capable, and—even, in some sense—creative.

Ultimately, whether we view AI agents as helpers, co-workers, or potentially disruptive forces, one point remains uncontroversial: their impact will be profound. As you turn the page, get ready to explore, question, and grapple with the brave new world of AI agents—and to shape your own informed perspective on a revolution in the making.

2

From Rules to Learning: The Evolution of Intelligent Systems

Artificial intelligence did not suddenly spring into existence at the moment modern machine learning techniques captured public attention. Rather, it has evolved through decades of research, trial and error, and numerous paradigm shifts. By understanding the roots of AI, we can better appreciate why today's AI agents—capable of learning, adapting, and making decisions in complex environments—represent such a significant milestone. This chapter will walk us through the most important transitions in AI's history: from early rule-based systems, which relied on explicit human-crafted instructions, to modern learning-based models that can discover patterns in data and refine themselves over time.

The Early Years: Symbolic Beginnings

The seeds of AI were planted in the mid-20th century, at a time when computers were still a relatively new invention. Researchers like Alan Turing, John McCarthy, Marvin Minsky, and others laid the conceptual groundwork by asking, "Can machines think?" Their initial approach was largely inspired by logic and mathematics. The belief was that if you provided a computer with rules of reasoning—just like a human might use formal logic—it could solve problems that typically required intelligence.

Often referred to as *symbolic AI* or *Good Old-Fashioned AI (GOFAI)*, this approach treated intelligence like a puzzle: you represent knowledge about a domain (for instance, medical diagnosis or chess) using symbols, and the computer applies logical operations to these symbols. One of the classic examples is the development of expert systems. An *expert system* is designed to mimic the decision-making abilities of a human expert, such as a doctor diagnosing a rare illness. It relies on a library of "if–then" rules: *If the patient has a fever and swollen glands, then check for infection. If the infection is of a certain type, prescribe antibiotics.* By chaining these rules together, the system could produce recommendations.

The promise of expert systems

During the 1970s and 1980s, expert systems thrived in niche areas like medical diagnostics, chemical analysis, and financial decision-making. Businesses liked them because they captured the know-how of top experts, making it easier for junior staff to make reasonably good decisions without always needing the expert on call. This technology sparked optimism: if all human knowledge could be broken down into logical rules, then computers could match human intellect, or so the reasoning went.

Yet symbolic AI had limitations. Writing out enough rules to capture the intricacies of real-world problems proved to be a monumental task. Humans often rely on intuition or "gut

..ing"—unspoken understandings that are hard to pin down in an if–then format. Moreover, real-world environments are messy: new conditions arise, or unexpected anomalies occur. Hard-coded rules can't easily adapt to situations outside of what their programmers anticipated. And as these systems scaled, they became cumbersome to maintain. This created a bottleneck that eventually sparked a major shift in AI research.

The First AI Winter and the Quest for Adaptability

Despite early excitement, the limitations of symbolic AI led to a period often referred to as the "AI Winter." Funding dried up as organizations realized that rule-based systems alone couldn't deliver on the wild predictions of achieving human-like intelligence. Computers excelled at meticulously following instructions but lacked the flexibility to handle new challenges without labor-intensive reprogramming.

Rethinking intelligence

Faced with these setbacks, some researchers began to propose a different approach: maybe we shouldn't try to encode every rule that governs intelligent behavior. Instead, we could let machines *learn* from examples, much like a child learns from interacting with the world. This idea had been around for some time—Frank Rosenblatt's *perceptron* model in the late 1950s was one of the earliest attempts to mimic how neurons in the human brain process information. Yet, due to technological and theoretical constraints, these early neural network models had limited success.

By the late 1980s and early 1990s, the concept of *machine learning* started to gain traction. Rather than exhaustively defining rules, researchers sought algorithms that improve automatically through experience. The arrival of more powerful computers and better mathematical tools made this feasible. The renaissance of neural networks, aided by the technique called **backpropagation**, allowed computers to adjust their internal parameters (akin to "weights" in a neural network) so that the system could better map inputs to desired outputs.

During this time, progress was still slow, partly because the datasets needed to train these algorithms were relatively small by today's standards, and computing power was limited. Nevertheless, the core principle—that a machine could *learn* from data rather than being explicitly programmed—was gaining momentum.

The Rise of Machine Learning and Data-Driven AI

As the internet expanded in the 1990s and early 2000s, data began to explode in availability. Online activity, digital sensors, e-commerce transactions, and social media posts suddenly offered massive amounts of information about how people behaved, what they liked, and what problems they needed to solve. Researchers recognized this goldmine and quickly developed machine learning techniques to harness such data. These techniques included:

1. **Supervised Learning:** Where an algorithm is given examples of inputs (e.g., images) paired with correct outputs (e.g., labels like "cat" or "dog"). The model adjusts itself to predict the correct label for each new image it encounters.
2. **Unsupervised Learning:** Where an algorithm tries to discover patterns in data without explicit labels—such as grouping similar items together or uncovering hidden

..es.

3. **Semi-Supervised and Self-Supervised Learning:** Methods that fall in between, making use of partial labels or leveraging the data itself to create training signals.

As more data became available, researchers found that machine learning could match or surpass human performance in certain tasks, like recognizing handwritten digits or detecting spam emails. This was a turning point, marking the birth of what many now call the *data-driven era* of AI.

Deep Learning breakthroughs

During the 2010s, what came to be known as *deep learning* built upon classic neural network ideas but utilized more complex architectures with multiple layers—these layers helped the system extract higher-order features automatically. With the support of powerful graphics processing units (GPUs) and specialized AI hardware, deep learning models achieved astonishing feats. Systems like AlexNet (2012) dramatically improved image recognition capabilities, while recurrent neural networks and transformer-based architectures advanced the state of the art in natural language processing. Suddenly, tasks like translating text between languages, transcribing speech, or generating coherent paragraphs became commonplace.

Importantly, these deep learning models weren't merely performing rigid computations. They used feedback loops from large datasets to *learn representations of the world.* Instead of a programmer telling the system, "Look for edges or corners," the system learned these features on its own. This was a leap forward in adaptability and is part of what paved the way for creating more intelligent, agent-based systems.

Reinforcement Learning: Beyond Static Data

While supervised and unsupervised learning propelled AI to new heights, they primarily operated on fixed datasets. In reality, many tasks require continuous interaction with an environment. This is where **reinforcement learning (RL)** comes into play—a technique that trains agents by rewarding them for desired actions and penalizing them for undesired ones.

The concept of RL can be likened to teaching a dog new tricks: when the dog does the right thing, it gets a treat; when it does the wrong thing, it doesn't. Over time, the dog associates certain behaviors with positive or negative outcomes and adapts accordingly. RL algorithms do something similar in a computational context. For instance:

- **Game playing:** RL systems became famously known through their successes in chess (Deep Blue, though that was more symbolic-based), Go (AlphaGo), and various Atari games. These agents learn not by being told which moves are correct, but by trying different strategies and discovering which sequences of moves maximize their chance of winning.
- **Robotics:** RL can also help robots learn how to walk, pick up objects, or navigate a maze. Instead of relying on an engineer to calculate the perfect motion path, the robot tries different actions. If it achieves its goal (e.g., successfully stacking blocks), it gets a reward signal.

This interactive process aligns well with the concept of AI agents. By definition, an agent perceives its environment, chooses an action, and experiences feedback (reward or lack thereof). Over many iterations, it refines its decision-making to better achieve its objectives.

Emergence of Multi-Agent Systems

The AI revolution didn't stop with single agents learning in isolation. Researchers soon realized that systems of multiple agents, each with their own objectives and perceptions, could lead to more complex, coordinated behaviors. This gave birth to the field of *multi-agent systems*. Imagine a group of drones coordinating to deliver medical supplies. Each drone has limited information about the environment, but by communicating with one another or sharing partial data, they can collectively figure out the best routes to ensure timely deliveries.

Multi-agent setups can also model competition. For instance, in scenarios like automated stock trading, multiple agents might each be trying to maximize their own returns. They essentially learn to anticipate and react to each other's strategies, which can produce emergent behavior that is more intricate and adaptive than what a single agent could manage. This capacity for emergent behavior is a key reason AI agents—especially in multi-agent contexts—hold so much promise for solving large-scale problems, from optimizing city traffic to coordinating supply chains.

The Path to AI Agents

So how do we connect these historical breakthroughs—symbolic rules, machine learning, deep learning, and reinforcement learning—to modern AI agents? The answer lies in *integration*:

1. **Combining Learning and Reasoning:** Many modern AI agents still incorporate symbolic logic for tasks that require domain-specific rules but are augmented by machine learning for tasks that require pattern recognition.
2. **Scalable Architectures:** Deep learning models with billions of parameters can now operate in real-time, thanks to faster computers, specialized chips, and optimized software libraries. This gives AI agents the raw horsepower to handle complex tasks.
3. **Continuous Feedback:** With reinforcement learning, agents no longer rely solely on static datasets. They can adapt to new information and unfamiliar situations, which is especially important for real-world deployments like self-driving cars or automated factories.
4. **Cloud and Edge Computing:** As internet connectivity becomes ubiquitous, AI agents can access vast amounts of data stored in the cloud, while also performing on-device computations (edge computing). This combination enables them to be both data-rich and responsive.

In effect, the modern AI agent is a product of multiple research strands converging. Symbolic AI contributes the ability to handle logic and rules. Machine learning provides a data-driven approach to discovering patterns. Deep learning unlocks complex perceptual tasks like vision and language understanding. And reinforcement learning offers a framework for continuous, interactive adaptation. *This synergy underpins the emergence of agents capable of navigating, deciding, and learning in real-time.*

Lessons from History

Understanding the timeline of AI evolution—its ups and downs—reminds us that innovation doesn't happen in a vacuum. Each wave of progress built upon earlier ideas, while also addressing the limitations that led to disillusionment (such as the AI Winter). This cyclical pattern offers several lessons:

- **Hype vs. Reality:** AI has gone through phases of intense hype followed by sobering realization. Current breakthroughs in AI agents are exciting, but we must remain grounded and aware of real-world constraints, such as the need for quality data and robust evaluation.
- **The Importance of Interdisciplinary Research:** Moving from rigid rules to adaptive learning involved mathematics, computer science, neuroscience, psychology, and other fields. This cross-pollination continues to drive AI forward.
- **Balancing Short-Term Gains with Long-Term Vision:** Technologies like machine learning provide commercial value quickly (through better recommendations, predictive analytics, etc.), but truly autonomous agents that solve broad, unscripted tasks demand ongoing research and collaboration.

Furthermore, history highlights that *societal factors*—funding priorities, market demand, ethical concerns—are just as important as technical breakthroughs. AI doesn't just live in labs; it intersects with politics, economics, and culture.

Relevance to the General Reader

Why should someone outside the tech industry care about these historical shifts from rules-based systems to learning-based approaches? Because these shifts inform the very capabilities and limitations of AI in our modern world. Today's AI agents owe their adaptability to the evolution of machine learning, their perceptual acumen to deep learning, and their capacity for decision-making to reinforcement learning. Understanding this background helps demystify the technology and makes it clearer why AI agents are not static tools but dynamic entities that "learn on the job."

For instance, if you're using a rideshare app, the app's pricing engine might be an AI agent that learns from supply and demand patterns, traffic data, and user behavior. If the system's calculations suddenly lead to surge pricing during a minor holiday, knowing that the AI relies heavily on historical data and real-time feedback might help you interpret that result more critically—or decide if it's worthwhile to wait for the prices to drop. On a broader scale, if your local city council is debating the deployment of AI-driven traffic lights or public safety measures, understanding that these systems are not merely "following rules" but rather constantly optimizing themselves can inform public discourse about accountability, error rates, and transparency.

Looking Ahead

Armed with this understanding of AI's evolution, we can now appreciate what makes AI agents fundamentally different: they are the sum of multiple decades of research and technological breakthroughs, capable of learning from their environment, adapting to new tasks, and even collaborating with or competing against other agents. In the chapters to come, we will delve deeper into the inner workings of these agents, the industries they're poised to revolutionize, and the ethical and societal considerations that accompany them.

Building from symbolic AI, through machine learning, to the advanced multi-agent systems of today, the history of AI is a tapestry of innovation, recalibration, and enduring ambition. Each shift not only added new capabilities but also raised new questions about accountability, fairness, and human involvement. And while the story of AI is far from over, this chapter provides crucial context for understanding where we are now—and where we might be headed.

As you turn the page, keep in mind that AI's journey from rules to learning is more than a technical narrative. It's a testament to humanity's drive to understand intelligence itself, to replicate it, and ultimately to extend it in ways that can help solve some of our most pressing challenges. But the further we push these boundaries, the more we must remain vigilant about the responsibilities and risks that come with creating systems that learn, adapt, and act in ways we might not always predict.

In Chapter 3, we will look "under the hood" of AI agents and unpack the key technologies that allow them to learn and make decisions. By exploring machine learning fundamentals, neural networks, and multi-agent dynamics, we'll gain a clearer picture of the complex machinery enabling AI agents to revolutionize our world. Whether you're intrigued by the history or concerned about the future, this journey through AI's origins sets the stage for a deeper dive into the architecture and operation of the intelligent systems that are reshaping our era.

3

Under the Hood: Key Technologies Driving AI Agents

From self-driving cars to digital assistants that anticipate our every need, AI agents operate in an astonishingly wide range of environments—and they often do so seamlessly. Yet many of us may wonder: *How do these systems actually work?* The "magic" of AI agents lies in a suite of core technologies that enable them to perceive the world, make decisions, and learn from experience. This chapter demystifies those technologies. We'll explore the basics of machine learning, delve into the neural networks that power today's most advanced AI, and then look at reinforcement learning, which allows agents to learn by trial and error in dynamic environments. By the end, you'll have a clearer understanding of the building blocks that bring AI agents to life.

1. The Foundations of Machine Learning

Before diving into the specifics, it helps to understand what machine learning (ML) is and why it's central to AI agents. In simplest terms, ML is a branch of artificial intelligence focused on enabling computers to learn patterns from data, rather than following only rigid, pre-programmed rules. When an AI agent uses ML, it doesn't rely on its human creators to tell it precisely how to respond in every situation; instead, it "discovers" what works best by analyzing examples or by interacting with an environment.

1.1 Data as the Driving Force

Data is the fuel that powers ML algorithms. Whether it's text from social media, sensor readings from an autonomous robot, or a database of labeled images, machine learning systems rely on real-world information to learn patterns and make predictions. The more relevant, high-quality data an algorithm has, the better it generally performs—though there can be diminishing returns if the data is noisy or redundant. This emphasis on data underpins many modern AI successes: platforms like Google and Facebook excel partly because they have massive datasets to train their models.

Why quantity isn't everything

More data doesn't always guarantee better outcomes. If the data is biased—say, a facial-recognition dataset that includes far more light-skinned faces than dark-skinned ones—an AI system can inherit and even amplify those biases. This highlights the importance of thoughtful data collection, validation, and curation. Quality data, combined with the right learning architecture, paves the way for robust AI agents.

1.2 The Three Major Learning Paradigms

Most machine learning methods fall into three broad categories:

1. **Supervised Learning:** The system learns from labeled examples. For instance, an image dataset where each photo is labeled as "cat" or "dog." By analyzing thousands (or millions) of such images, the model identifies features that distinguish these animals. Once trained, it can classify new, unseen images with considerable accuracy.
2. **Unsupervised Learning:** Here, the data is not labeled. The system's goal is to find structure in the data—for example, grouping customers by purchasing habits or identifying similarities in user behavior without knowing the "right" categories in advance. Unsupervised methods are invaluable for discovering hidden patterns that might not be obvious to human analysts.
3. **Reinforcement Learning (RL):** This paradigm is particularly relevant for AI agents. Instead of learning from a static dataset, the agent interacts with an environment, receiving rewards or penalties based on its actions. Over time, it refines its strategy to maximize rewards. We'll discuss RL in greater detail later in the chapter.

2. Neural Networks: The Brains of Modern AI

While symbolic AI once dominated the field (as discussed in Chapter 2), the resurgence of neural networks has been the game-changer driving most contemporary breakthroughs.

Artificial neural networks are computational models inspired by the structure of the human brain. They consist of layers of interconnected "neurons," each of which transforms its inputs and passes them on to the next layer.

2.1 The Basics of Neural Networks

Think of a single artificial neuron as a very simple calculator that takes several inputs, multiplies them by weights, sums everything up, and then applies an activation function to decide what signal to send onward. A network of these neurons forms a complex function that can approximate a huge range of input–output relationships.

1. **Input Layer:** Receives the raw data (e.g., pixel values in an image).
2. **Hidden Layers:** Transform the input data through multiple stages, extracting and combining features. The number and size of these layers often determines how "deep" the network is.
3. **Output Layer:** Produces the final prediction or classification (e.g., cat vs. dog).

Each neuron's weights (and sometimes biases) get updated during training. For supervised tasks, this update process typically uses an algorithm called **backpropagation**, which adjusts the weights to minimize the difference between the model's predictions and the actual labels.

2.2 Deep Learning Architectures

The term "deep learning" usually refers to neural networks with multiple hidden layers. These layers allow the network to learn *hierarchical* representations of data. For instance, in image processing, early layers might detect edges and simple shapes, while deeper layers capture more complex patterns like textures or facial features. A few types of architectures stand out:

- **Convolutional Neural Networks (CNNs):** Especially good at image-related tasks. Their convolutional layers act like filters, scanning images to detect local features such as edges or corners.
- **Recurrent Neural Networks (RNNs):** Designed to handle sequential data like text or time series. Variants like LSTM (Long Short-Term Memory) help manage long-term dependencies in sequences, making them powerful for language modeling and speech recognition.
- **Transformers:** A more recent and immensely popular architecture that has revolutionized natural language processing. Transformers excel at capturing relationships between words (or other tokens) across an entire sequence without needing to process data strictly in order. This has led to advanced language models capable of writing essays, translating languages, and even composing poetry.

Why depth matters

Deeper networks can learn more abstract features, but they also require significantly more data and computational resources. Training these models used to be prohibitively expensive, but the rise of Graphics Processing Units (GPUs), specialized AI chips (like tensor processing units), and cloud computing has made large-scale training feasible. These hardware advancements have been as critical as the algorithmic innovations themselves.

3. Reinforcement Learning: Agents That Learn by Doing

So far, we've touched on *supervised* and *unsupervised* learning, which rely on historical or static datasets. But many AI agents learn through **reinforcement learning (RL)**, a technique that mimics the way humans (and animals) learn from experience.

3.1 How RL Works

In RL, an agent interacts with an environment step by step. After each action, the agent receives a *reward signal*, which could be positive or negative. Its goal is to maximize the cumulative reward over time. This approach is particularly powerful in scenarios where:

- **The agent doesn't have labeled examples** for every possible situation.
- **The environment is dynamic and changes** based on the agent's actions (or other factors).
- **Feedback is delayed**, meaning the agent might only see the result of its actions well after it has made them.

Consider a self-driving car as an RL agent. Each time it negotiates a turn or merges into traffic without incident, it effectively "learns" that careful steering and speed adjustments lead to a positive outcome (staying on the road safely). If it attempts a risky maneuver and almost causes an accident, it "realizes" that such actions lead to negative feedback. Over countless simulated or real-world driving episodes, the car refines its policy (i.e., its strategy for choosing actions) to navigate more safely and efficiently.

3.2 Breakthroughs in RL

One of the most publicized RL achievements came from **AlphaGo**, developed by DeepMind. Using a combination of deep neural networks and advanced search algorithms, AlphaGo learned to play the board game Go at a superhuman level. The idea was simple yet profound: rather than analyzing every possible board state (which is astronomically large in Go), the system learned patterns through practice games against itself, refining its strategy with each iteration.

Similarly, DeepMind's **AlphaZero** generalized this approach to excel at multiple games, including chess and Shogi. Beyond the realm of gaming, RL techniques are now applied in robotics (for tasks like grasping and locomotion), resource allocation (e.g., scheduling servers in data centers), and personalized recommendations (optimizing the "reward" of user engagement).

4. Multi-Agent Systems: When AI Agents Work Together

While reinforcement learning is often described from the perspective of a single agent, real-world problems frequently involve multiple agents that either cooperate or compete—or both. This brings us to **multi-agent systems**:

- **Cooperative Systems:** Agents share information and work toward a collective goal. An example is a team of autonomous drones coordinating to survey farmland or deliver medical supplies to remote areas.
- **Competitive Systems:** Agents are designed to maximize their own reward at the possible expense of others. Stock-trading bots on Wall Street fall into this category, each trying to "outsmart" the market and other bots.

Researchers have found that when agents learn in groups, they can develop complex behaviors that sometimes **emerge** from simple rules and interactions. Just as bird flocks can show intricate flight patterns without centralized control, multi-agent AI systems can manifest strategies that go beyond what any single agent would do independently. This emergent intelligence is one reason multi-agent RL is a vibrant area of current research.

5. Explainability and Transparency: Looking Inside the "Black Box"

Modern AI agents—particularly deep learning models—are often criticized for being **black boxes**. Their internal workings can be so complex that even the engineers who build them struggle to explain why they reach certain decisions. This opacity raises concerns:

1. **Trust:** In high-stakes domains like healthcare or aviation, decisions made by an AI agent can have life-or-death implications. Stakeholders want clear rationales.
2. **Accountability:** When an AI agent denies a loan application

or diagnoses a medical condition, regulators and users increasingly demand to know *why* it made that choice.

3. **Bias and Fairness:** If an agent inadvertently discriminates against certain groups, we need a means to diagnose and correct such biases.

5.1 Efforts Toward Explainable AI (XAI)

Researchers are actively developing methods to interpret AI outputs. Techniques range from visualizing which parts of an image a convolutional network deems important, to generating "saliency maps" that highlight the variables most influential in a decision. In the context of language models, tools can identify which words or phrases in a sentence drive the model's response.

Another approach is to build simpler, more interpretable models—like decision trees or linear models—around the larger neural network, giving approximate explanations of its behavior. While these methods are a step forward, achieving truly transparent AI agents that rival human intuition in clarity remains an open challenge.

6. The Vital Role of Infrastructure

Having cutting-edge algorithms is only half the story. Today's AI agents also depend on **robust computing infrastructure**:

- **Cloud Computing:** Offers scalable, on-demand access to powerful hardware. Organizations can spin up hundreds of GPU-powered servers to train a large neural network and then scale back down once training completes.

- **Edge Computing:** Moves the computation closer to where data is generated—like on a smartphone or IoT device—reducing latency and improving privacy (since data doesn't need to travel to the cloud).
- **APIs and Frameworks:** Libraries like TensorFlow, PyTorch, and scikit-learn provide pre-built functionalities that simplify model building. This means developers don't have to reinvent the wheel each time they implement neural networks or reinforcement learning algorithms.

Why it matters

This infrastructure democratizes AI research and development. Startups and academic researchers can rent powerful hardware in the cloud without needing their own supercomputers. Meanwhile, user-facing applications like real-time language translation or on-device voice assistants benefit from edge processing that's fast and efficient. These factors significantly influence how quickly AI agents can be deployed across industries—from healthcare and finance to retail and transportation.

7. Balancing Complexity and Practicality

AI agents represent the fusion of multiple advanced technologies, but real-world deployments must also consider constraints like cost, reliability, safety, and ease of use. For example, while a large neural network might deliver superior accuracy, it may be too large and energy-intensive to run on a consumer device. Or, a highly dynamic multi-agent system might be too unpredictable for certain safety-critical tasks.

Why simpler solutions sometimes win

In some cases, a more modest machine learning approach—like a smaller neural network or even a rule-based system—may be perfectly adequate for a given problem. For instance, a chatbot that helps reset passwords might not require the sophistication of a huge language model. It needs only to handle specific queries reliably, which can be done with simpler algorithms that are cheaper to train and easier to maintain.

8. Making It All Accessible to the General Reader

If you're not a technical professional, terms like "neural networks," "reinforcement learning," and "transformers" can feel daunting. However, here's how you can contextualize them in everyday life:

- **Neural Networks** are what power the face-recognition feature on your smartphone camera. Each time you unlock your phone, the camera's neural network quickly matches your face to the one stored in memory.
- **Reinforcement Learning** is behind some recommendation engines that adapt to your preferences over time, even as those preferences shift. It also underlies advanced robotics, which might learn to grasp objects by repeated trial and error.
- **Transformers** drive cutting-edge chatbots and language tools. When you use an online translator or type a message that's auto-completed with surprising accuracy, you're likely interacting with a Transformer-based model.

By connecting these concepts to your own experiences—an image that's automatically tagged, a website that knows what you want to buy, a vacuum robot that learns your floor plan—the underpinnings of AI feel less abstract. You begin to see that these are not impenetrable black boxes from a science-fiction movie, but carefully engineered systems fueled by data, algorithms, and vast computing power.

9. The Road Ahead

As AI agents continue to evolve, the interplay of these foundational technologies will become even more intricate. We may see more sophisticated **hybrid models**, where symbolic logic (rules) is fused with deep learning. Advanced reinforcement learning techniques might one day guide entire fleets of autonomous vehicles, communicating in real-time to prevent accidents and reduce traffic congestion. Multi-agent systems could transform industries like finance, where trading bots "cooperate" to stabilize markets or, conversely, "compete" in new ways that require regulatory oversight.

Hardware acceleration will also keep pace, enabling more advanced neural network architectures that were once purely theoretical. Meanwhile, demands for transparency and fairness will push researchers to develop new forms of explainable AI, ensuring that users, policymakers, and other stakeholders can trust the decisions AI agents make on their behalf.

10. Key Takeaways

1. **Machine Learning:** The broader umbrella that lets computers learn from data, divided into supervised, unsupervised, and reinforcement learning.
2. **Neural Networks and Deep Learning:** The primary drivers

of modern AI advances, enabling pattern recognition that surpasses traditional methods in fields like image classification and language processing.

3. **Reinforcement Learning:** Especially important for AI agents that must navigate and act within dynamic environments, learning from feedback in real time.
4. **Multi-Agent Systems:** When multiple agents either cooperate or compete, we see emergent behaviors that can tackle complex, large-scale problems—or introduce new complexities.
5. **Infrastructure Matters:** Without powerful hardware, cloud computing, and robust frameworks, these technologies would remain confined to research labs.
6. **Explainability and Ethics:** As AI agents become more integral to society, we need transparent models that can be held accountable.

11. Conclusion

The world of AI agents is a fascinating tapestry woven from various threads of technology—machine learning, deep neural networks, reinforcement learning, multi-agent coordination, and more. Each thread contributes a specific capability: pattern recognition, adaptive decision-making, or collaboration at scale. When combined, they give rise to agents that can handle tasks previously thought to be exclusive to human intelligence.

Understanding these underlying technologies, even at a conceptual level, is increasingly important for anyone navigating the digital age. It helps demystify AI's capabilities and limitations, fosters informed discussions around ethical deployment, and empowers you—whether as a citizen, consumer, or professional—to engage with AI in a meaningful way. Far from being arcane tools that only PhD-level scientists can grasp, the building blocks of AI are accessible to anyone willing to explore the logic and learning processes behind them.

In the next chapter, we'll focus on the diverse applications of AI agents across industries—from healthcare and finance to manufacturing and beyond. We'll see how these core technologies, once mere lab experiments, are reshaping workflows, reconfiguring value chains, and inspiring new business models in the process. By the end of that exploration, the momentum behind AI agents' global impact will become even clearer—and so will the profound societal shifts that may follow.

4

Types of AI Agents

Picture an automated chatbot that pops up on your favorite shopping website, ready to answer your questions in real time. Now compare that to a self-driving car carefully plotting the safest route through unpredictable city traffic. Although they both rely on artificial intelligence (AI), these two examples operate in profoundly different ways. That diversity is captured in the concept of "AI agents," each type distinguished by how it perceives the world, processes information, and makes decisions. In this chapter, we'll examine the different types of AI agents—*Reactive, Deliberative/Cognitive, Hybrid*, and *Specialized vs. Generalized*—highlighting why these distinctions matter for real-world applications.

1. Why Classifying Agents Matters

Not every AI agent learns or acts in the same way. Some respond almost instantly to the environment without extensive internal reasoning, while others maintain a detailed model of the world, planning multiple steps ahead. Some are designed to excel at one task, whereas others aim for broader capabilities. Understanding these categories helps us grasp the trade-offs in autonomy, adaptability, and complexity. Whether you're developing AI systems for business or simply using them in daily life, knowing these differences sheds light on why certain agents work the way they do—and why some are better suited for specific tasks than others.

2. Reactive Agents: Quick and Targeted

Reactive agents are the simplest form of AI agents. They take in sensory inputs (or data inputs) from the environment and immediately produce an output or action based on a set of rules or learned policies. There's no memory of past states beyond what's needed to handle the current situation, and there's no deep internal model of the future. Essentially, a reactive agent is always living "in the now," making decisions in real time.

2.1 How Reactive Agents Operate

The hallmark of a reactive agent is its direct mapping from *situation* to *action*. In other words, it perceives something—say, a sudden obstacle in front of a vacuum robot—and reacts by executing a predefined or learned response (turn away, slow down, stop). These agents typically don't speculate about *why* the obstacle is there or *what* might happen next; they just follow their immediate instructions or learned behavior for that particular scenario.

For example, many basic chatbots can be considered reactive: they might trigger responses based on keyword detection or simple decision trees. Once they identify the presence of a certain keyword (e.g., "returns" on a retail website), they respond with a specific script about how to initiate a product return.

2.2 Advantages and Disadvantages of Reactive Agents

- **Advantages:**

1. **Speed:** Because there's no extensive deliberation process, reactive agents can be lightning-fast. This makes them ideal for real-time applications where latency is a concern (e.g., streaming data analysis, simple game-playing bots).
2. **Simplicity:** They are easier to design and maintain. If the environment is relatively stable or if you only need the agent to handle well-defined tasks, a reactive approach may suffice.

- **Disadvantages:**

1. **Lack of Context:** Reactive agents typically lack memory or the ability to plan for future scenarios. This can make them brittle when facing unexpected changes in the environment.
2. **Limited Adaptability:** Without an internal model or the ability to learn from past experiences, reactive agents struggle to improve performance over time or adapt to novel, complex tasks.

2.3 Common Use Cases

- **Spam Filters:** Many email spam detectors are, at their core, reactive. They look for known spam indicators (keywords, suspicious links) and filter emails accordingly, without deeper context.
- **Basic Robotics:** A simple line-following robot that tracks a black strip on the floor is the epitome of a reactive system.
- **Automated Customer Support Chatbots:** Though increasingly these systems also incorporate some machine learning, the simpler versions respond with canned answers based on user queries or keywords.

Reactive agents work best in stable or predictable settings where swift, direct responses are both sufficient and desirable. While they lack the sophistication to learn extensively or plan ahead, their speed and simplicity can be invaluable in many domains.

3. Deliberative (Cognitive) Agents: Think Before You Act

While reactive agents respond immediately to the environment, *deliberative* or *cognitive* agents maintain an internal model of their world, reason about it, and use that reasoning to plan future actions. They are designed to mimic more closely how humans approach complex problem-solving: we gather information, process it using mental models or knowledge, and then choose a course of action with some foresight.

3.1 Internal Models and Reasoning

Deliberative agents construct or maintain a representation of their environment and their own internal states. This can involve:

1. **State Estimation:** Keeping track of the current situation (e.g., a self-driving car's location, its speed, nearby vehicles).
2. **Goal and Plan Formulation:** Identifying objectives (e.g., "reach the destination safely" or "achieve checkmate in chess") and devising a strategy to reach them.
3. **Decision Making:** Selecting an optimal or near-optimal action based on predicted outcomes.

Because deliberative agents rely on models and predictions, they can handle more complex, less predictable domains. They can also incorporate learning processes that refine their models over time, making them increasingly effective.

3.2 The Power of Planning

A key advantage of deliberative agents is *planning*. Rather than reacting to events as they unfold, these agents can simulate various courses of action and choose the best one in advance. This is especially useful in settings where an action has long-term consequences or where mistakes are costly.

- **Robotics:** A household robot might plan a sequence of moves to finish cleaning a room in the most efficient order—starting near the door to avoid spreading dirt over already-cleaned areas.

- **Transportation:** Self-driving cars rely heavily on predictive models, anticipating other vehicles' behaviors and adjusting their own route or speed accordingly.

3.3 Challenges for Deliberative Agents

Despite their sophistication, deliberative agents face a few notable challenges:

1. **Computational Complexity:** Maintaining and updating a detailed world model requires substantial computing power, especially in dynamic or large-scale environments.
2. **Handling Uncertainty:** No model is perfect. Agents must deal with incomplete or noisy information. Overconfidence in a flawed model can lead to poor decisions.
3. **Time Constraints:** The planning process can take time. In rapidly changing environments (like real-world traffic), an agent must balance the benefits of planning with the risk of becoming too slow to act effectively.

4. Hybrid Agents: Best of Both Worlds

Many real-world systems blend *reactive* and *deliberative* approaches to form **hybrid agents**. This strategy acknowledges that exclusively reactive agents can be too simplistic for complex tasks, while purely deliberative agents can be slow or overly resource-intensive.

4.1 Layered Architectures

A common design for hybrid agents is to use a layered architecture, such as:

1. **Reactive Layer:** Operates at the "ground level," handling immediate actions that need quick responses (e.g., obstacle avoidance in a robot).
2. **Deliberative Layer:** Works in parallel or in stages, creating long-term plans and strategies (e.g., route planning).
3. **Coordination or Executive Layer:** Manages interactions between the reactive and deliberative layers, deciding when to rely on one or the other.

For instance, consider a drone delivering packages in a busy city. The reactive layer might ensure it avoids collisions with buildings or birds, while the deliberative layer plans the most efficient path to reach the destination. The executive layer balances both: if a sudden gust of wind pushes the drone off course, the reactive layer quickly adjusts its flight, but the deliberative layer recalculates the overall route to compensate.

4.2 Advantages of Hybrid Agents

1. **Robustness:** By combining fast reactions with thoughtful planning, hybrid agents are more adaptable to unexpected changes without losing sight of broader objectives.
2. **Scalability:** Different layers can be developed and improved somewhat independently. Engineers can focus on enhancing the reactive subsystem's accuracy while simultaneously refining the deliberative planner.

4.3 Real-World Examples

- **Advanced Robotics:** Many cutting-edge robots, from warehouse pick-and-place machines to humanoid robots, use hybrid architectures. They can react instantaneously to avoid dropping an object while still following a planned sequence of tasks.
- **Autonomous Vehicles:** Self-driving systems commonly run multiple layers simultaneously—fusing sensor data in real time to avoid hazards (reactive) while mapping and re-mapping routes (deliberative).

Hybrid agents demonstrate that "either/or" isn't the only approach. By carefully combining the strengths of different methodologies, these systems offer both agility and foresight—an especially valuable mix in complex environments.

5. Specialized vs. Generalized Agents

Beyond how agents reason about their environments, another critical dimension is *scope*. Some AI agents are meticulously engineered for one particular job, while others aim for broader, more flexible intelligence.

5.1 Narrow (Specialized) Agents

Most of today's powerful AI systems are "narrow" or "specialized" agents. They excel in specific domains but lack the versatility to generalize across wildly different tasks. For instance:

- **Chess Engines:** AlphaZero can utterly dominate human grandmasters in chess or Go but can't drive a car or hold a conversation about politics.
- **Voice Assistants:** Siri and Alexa can handle voice commands effectively but won't be designing complex financial models or diagnosing rare diseases.

Despite their focus, specialized agents have revolutionized industries. They're often cheaper to train, easier to deploy, and more reliable in their defined tasks than a more general system that tries to do everything at once.

5.2 Toward Generalized Agents

In contrast, the idea of a *generalized agent* (sometimes called "Artificial General Intelligence" or AGI) is to create an AI that can handle a wide array of tasks, much like a human can learn new skills. While we haven't yet achieved true AGI, researchers are gradually pushing the boundaries with large language models and multi-modal systems that can handle text, images, and other input types together.

- **Large Language Models (LLMs):** Tools like GPT have demonstrated remarkable adaptability, from writing essays and poetry to summarizing complex articles. Though still not "fully general," these systems hint at the possibilities of broader AI capabilities.
- **Multi-Agent Collaboration:** In some scenarios, multiple specialized agents can work together in a framework that approximates more generalized abilities. For example, one agent might handle complex calculations, another handles

language translation, and a third navigates a physical environment. Combined, they perform tasks that seem far more general.

5.3 Trade-Offs Between Specialized and Generalized

- **Performance:** Specialized agents often achieve higher performance in their domain of expertise than a generalized system that tries to do multiple tasks.
- **Flexibility:** A generalized agent can adapt to multiple tasks but might not reach the same peak performance in any single area.
- **Resource Requirements:** The more generalized a system aims to be, the more computational resources, data, and engineering effort it typically requires.

For now, most practical AI solutions remain specialized, but the allure of building a more universal intelligence continues to drive research. Whether or not we'll see a true AGI soon remains a hotly debated topic.

6. Choosing the Right Agent for the Job

With such diversity among agents—reactive, deliberative, hybrid, specialized, and generalized—how do we decide which approach works best? The answer usually depends on:

1. **Task Complexity:** Simple tasks (like classifying emails as spam or not) often only need a reactive agent or a specialized model. More complex tasks (like coordinating multiple drones in unpredictable weather) benefit from

deliberation or a hybrid system.

2. **Performance Requirements:** If real-time speed is crucial (e.g., collision avoidance), a reactive component is essential. If planning and optimization matter (e.g., scheduling cargo in a global logistics network), a deliberative or hybrid design is favored.
3. **Environment Stability:** In a stable environment, you can rely more on prior knowledge and planning. In a highly dynamic or uncertain environment, adaptability—whether reactive or learning-based—becomes paramount.
4. **Resources and Expertise:** Building a sophisticated deliberative or hybrid agent can be complex and costly. It might also require specialized teams of data scientists, roboticists, or software engineers.

7. Illustrative Real-World Scenarios

Scenario 1: Warehouse Robot

A warehouse wants to automate item retrieval. Each day, a robot must pick different items off the shelves and deliver them to a packing station. Here's how different types of agents might approach the job:

- **Reactive Agent:** Might continuously scan for barcodes matching the current pick list, retrieving items on a nearest-first basis with no broader strategy. It works well when everything is labeled correctly and items are always in predictable locations.
- **Deliberative Agent:** Maintains a map of the warehouse, calculates optimal routes, and plans picking sequences to

minimize travel time. It might also predict when shelves will need restocking based on historical patterns.
- **Hybrid Agent:** Combines quick obstacle avoidance (reactive) with strategic route planning (deliberative). This ensures the robot can handle unexpected obstructions (like another robot or a misplaced pallet) without losing sight of its efficiency goals.

Scenario 2: Personal Finance Assistant

Imagine an AI-driven app that manages your budget, pays bills, and invests leftover funds:

- **Reactive Agent:** Might only respond to certain triggers, such as an overdraft alert, and send you a notification. It's straightforward but doesn't anticipate future cash flow.
- **Deliberative Agent:** Projects future expenses, models investment returns, and creates a monthly plan to optimize your savings. It's more powerful but needs more data and processing to model your financial world accurately.
- **Hybrid Agent:** Could do both: respond instantly to unusual transactions or low balances (reactive) while also running a broader financial plan in the background (deliberative). This combination ensures day-to-day vigilance plus long-term goal management.

8. Implications for the General Reader

As AI agents become more integrated into everything from household appliances to online customer service, it helps to recognize that not all agents are alike. If you're using a reactive chatbot, you might notice it fails to recall the context of previous messages. A more deliberative assistant might adapt to your conversation style, but it could also feel slower or occasionally overcomplicate its responses.

Moreover, these differences matter when it comes to **trust** and **expectations**. A purely reactive system might be perfect for immediate tasks but could make confounding mistakes if asked to handle more nuanced scenarios. Conversely, a cognitively advanced agent could appear highly capable in many respects yet become unpredictable in edge cases. Understanding these distinctions helps set realistic expectations for AI technology and fosters informed discussions about its deployment in sensitive areas like healthcare, finance, or education.

9. Where Are We Headed?

Looking ahead, the line between these agent types might blur further. Hybrid systems are already the norm for many advanced applications, and new breakthroughs in large language models and multi-modal systems may allow more general functionality within specialized domains.

In future chapters, we will see how these different agent types are deployed across industries. For instance, in healthcare, certain AI tools are purely reactive—flagging abnormal test results—while others are deliberative, formulating treatment plans by analyzing patient data over time. In financial services, we'll learn how AI agents run complex trading algorithms that shift between quick, reactive decisions and more extensive modeling of market trends. Each industry's unique demands will favor certain agent designs over others.

10. Key Takeaways

1. **Reactive Agents** respond immediately based on the current environment, offering speed and simplicity but limited adaptability.
2. **Deliberative (Cognitive) Agents** build internal models and plan ahead, enabling nuanced decision-making but requiring more computational resources and careful design.
3. **Hybrid Agents** combine reactive and deliberative elements, striking a balance between agility and foresight.
4. **Specialized Agents** excel in a narrow domain but may lack the ability to transfer their skills elsewhere.
5. **Generalized Agents** aspire to broader capabilities, though true AGI remains a long-term research challenge.

Understanding these categories is crucial not just for technologists but for anyone interacting with AI in daily life. Whether you're asking a virtual assistant to turn on your lights or relying on an automated system to guide your car through traffic, the underlying agent design shapes your experience.

In Closing

Just as human intelligence manifests in countless forms—some of us are quick reactors, others are meticulous planners—AI agents, too, span a spectrum of abilities and approaches. Reactive agents handle rapid-fire tasks, deliberative ones excel at planning, and hybrids aim for the best of both worlds. Meanwhile, specialized agents target narrow tasks with impressive performance, and the dream of a generalized intelligence continues to push the frontiers of research.

With this map of the AI agent landscape, you're better equipped to appreciate the variety of solutions powering modern life. In the next chapter, we'll zoom out to see where these agents are making the most impact—healthcare, finance, manufacturing, and beyond. You'll discover concrete examples of how AI agents are reshaping entire industries, often behind the scenes, and what that means for businesses, workers, and consumers alike. By seeing how the theoretical distinctions play out in practice, we'll further understand the full scope and scale of the AI revolution currently unfolding around us.

5

AI Agents in Action: Transforming Industries

Around the world, AI agents are entering workplaces, hospitals, factories, and city streets—often quietly and behind the scenes. While previous chapters explored the foundations and types of AI agents, this chapter focuses on real-world deployments that highlight how these systems transform entire industries. From helping doctors diagnose illnesses to powering autonomous vehicles, AI agents are already changing business models, improving efficiency, and sparking debates about the future of work. Whether you're a casual observer, an industry professional, or simply curious about what's ahead, understanding these applications provides concrete insight into just how impactful AI agents can be.

1. The Broad Reach of AI Agents

It's tempting to think that AI's most significant strides are limited to a few high-tech domains. Yet AI agents are increasingly woven into the fabric of everyday life. In factories, they track inventory and quality control; in finance, they monitor transactions for fraud in real time; in retail, they serve as virtual sales assistants that can upsell products tailored to a customer's profile. This broad reach stems from the adaptability of AI agents—their capacity to learn from data, respond to changing environments, and collaborate with or even replace older software systems that once relied on static rules.

Crucially, the adoption of AI agents tends to accelerate once an industry recognizes the competitive edge that automation and predictive analytics can bring. As more companies see positive returns on investment, AI's presence only grows. With that, of course, come questions about privacy, transparency, and the potential reshaping of entire job categories. These issues will be explored later, but first, let's look at where AI agents are already creating value in five major sectors: healthcare, finance, manufacturing, transportation, and retail/e-commerce.

2. Healthcare: From Diagnoses to Personalized Treatment

2.1 Diagnostic Support and Medical Imaging

AI agents in healthcare often appear as diagnostic support tools. These systems can quickly process a massive volume of medical images—like X-rays, CT scans, or MRIs—and highlight areas that deserve a radiologist's attention. By learning to recognize subtle indicators of disease (for instance, minuscule lung nodules that may signal early-stage cancer), these agents aim to reduce human error and expedite patient care.

In some hospitals, AI-driven imaging agents already serve as a second line of review, catching abnormalities that might be overlooked in a fast-paced environment. This doesn't eliminate the need for radiologists—on the contrary, it *augments* their work. Doctors can focus on complex judgments and patient interaction, rather than sifting through hundreds of scans each day.

2.2 Virtual Health Assistants

Chatbots and symptom-checker applications have evolved into AI agents that offer preliminary medical advice. Although these tools do not replace a trained physician, they can help triage patients by recommending whether to schedule an in-person consultation or try home care. Some advanced agents integrate with wearable devices, analyzing metrics like heart rate, sleep patterns, and even blood oxygen levels to offer personalized wellness tips.

For those managing chronic conditions such as diabetes or hypertension, AI agents can monitor real-time data, send medication reminders, and alert healthcare providers if readings enter a dangerous range. This continuous virtual care can reduce hospital visits and help patients stay on track with their treatment plans.

2.3 Personalized Treatment Plans

Combining medical records, genomic data, and real-time patient information, certain AI agents assist doctors in formulating treatment strategies. By comparing an individual's health profile to large datasets, these systems can suggest which interventions—like a specific chemotherapy regimen—have historically produced the best results for patients with similar characteristics.

While still in its infancy, personalized medicine holds the promise of more efficient, targeted care. As more data is collected and algorithms improve, these AI agents could become invaluable in reducing trial-and-error in treatments, especially for complex diseases like cancer or autoimmune conditions.

3. Finance: Fraud Detection, Trading, and Beyond

3.1 Real-Time Fraud Detection

The financial sector was among the earliest adopters of AI, largely because of the high stakes involved in fraud and risk assessment. In the past, rule-based systems detected anomalies like suspicious credit card purchases by matching transactions against known patterns. Modern AI agents, armed with machine learning, can analyze each incoming transaction in real time, comparing it to the customer's history and broader spending trends. If something appears unusual—like an expensive purchase in a foreign country—the system flags or blocks the transaction and notifies the bank.

These fraud-detection agents rely heavily on data analysis. They learn from every transaction and continuously update their models to keep pace with criminals' evolving tactics. The result is a more proactive approach, catching fraud earlier and reducing false alarms.

3.2 Algorithmic and High-Frequency Trading

Stock market trading provides a classic example of how AI agents can transform an entire domain. High-frequency trading (HFT) algorithms execute trades in fractions of a second, scanning market data for fleeting opportunities. More sophisticated AI agents incorporate *reinforcement learning* and *natural language processing* to gauge market sentiment and news headlines, attempting to predict short-term price movements before others do.

Although profitable for some, these strategies have attracted criticism for increasing market volatility and giving well-funded firms an advantage over retail investors. The role of AI agents here demonstrates how technology can alter competitive dynamics—sometimes in ways that challenge existing regulations.

3.3 Personal Financial Management

On the consumer side, AI agents also appear in user-facing apps that help individuals manage their budgets, investments, and loans. For instance, a digital assistant might analyze one's spending habits and recommend areas to cut back on or find better interest rates for savings. Some advanced budgeting tools even simulate future scenarios, offering personalized advice on insurance needs, retirement planning, or loan repayment schedules. These agents bridge the gap between professional financial planners and those who might not have access to personalized services, democratizing financial literacy and guidance.

4. Manufacturing: Automation and Intelligent Supply Chains

4.1 Robotic Process Automation and Quality Assurance

Manufacturers have been integrating robots into assembly lines for decades. However, the emergence of **AI agents** adds a new layer of intelligence to these robots. Instead of merely repeating preset motions, a factory robot can now adapt its actions in real time. For instance, it might detect a slight defect in a product component and adjust its grip to avoid breakage, or even alert a human supervisor if too many defects appear—a potential sign of an upstream problem.

Some factories use automated camera systems (also driven by AI agents) to conduct real-time quality checks. Any deviation from the expected product specifications triggers an alert, allowing for faster intervention. This reduces waste, lowers costs, and can significantly improve overall product consistency.

4.2 Predictive Maintenance

Traditional maintenance schedules follow rigid timetables: machines get serviced or replaced at fixed intervals, whether they need it or not. AI agents can overhaul this approach by analyzing sensor data—temperature, vibration levels, output quality, and more—to predict when a machine will fail or require tuning. This technique, known as **predictive maintenance**, enables just-in-time repairs, minimizing downtime and avoiding costly breakdowns.

Manufacturers often deploy a network of sensors throughout a plant, feeding real-time data into an AI system. Over time, the agent learns the "normal" operating patterns of each piece of equipment and flags anomalies. This not only saves money but also increases operational safety, preventing accidents that could occur if machinery fails unexpectedly.

4.3 Intelligent Supply Chain Management

From raw materials to finished goods, managing a global supply chain is complex. AI agents can optimize inventory levels, forecast demand, and reroute shipments in response to disruptions like natural disasters or port closures. By integrating data from multiple sources—logistics networks, customer orders, and even weather forecasts—these agents can make near-instant adjustments, ensuring that materials and products flow smoothly along the chain.

Large-scale companies, like Amazon and Walmart, have invested heavily in AI-driven supply chain solutions. The result is faster shipping, fewer stock-outs, and potentially lower prices for consumers. Yet it also underscores how reliant modern businesses are on automated decision-making—a single glitch in an AI system can ripple across thousands of miles of supply routes.

5. Transportation: Autonomous Vehicles and Smarter Logistics

5.1 Self-Driving Cars and Public Transit

Autonomous vehicles are among the most visible, talked-about examples of AI in action. These agents interpret data from cameras, LIDAR, radar, and GPS to navigate roads and make split-second decisions. **Reactive** components handle urgent tasks like obstacle avoidance, while **deliberative** layers plan routes, taking into account traffic patterns and road conditions. When multiple cars connect to a central network—or communicate vehicle-to-vehicle—multi-agent coordination can further optimize traffic flows and reduce congestion.

The promise is huge: fewer accidents caused by human error, more efficient traffic patterns, and new mobility options for those unable to drive. However, significant technical, regulatory, and ethical hurdles remain. Ensuring that autonomous vehicles behave safely in every possible scenario is a monumental challenge, and local laws vary widely on what's permissible for testing and deployment.

5.2 Fleet Management and Logistics

Even if self-driving vehicles remain partially restricted for now, AI agents still streamline transportation logistics. Companies use them to schedule deliveries, optimize routes for truck fleets, and even analyze driver behavior. By minimizing fuel consumption and time spent idling in traffic, these systems can reduce both operational costs and carbon footprints.

For ride-hailing services like Uber or Lyft, AI agents match riders to drivers, set dynamic prices, and predict demand surges. While beneficial to operational efficiency, dynamic pricing often sparks controversy—passengers may see sharply rising fares at peak times, which raises questions about fairness and consumer protection. Nonetheless, these pricing agents exemplify how AI can handle real-time resource allocation in a fluid marketplace.

6. Retail and E-Commerce: Personalization and Inventory Optimization

6.1 Recommendation Systems

Have you ever noticed how streaming services always seem to know which movie you'd enjoy next, or how online shops serve up items that match your preferences? These are the work of AI-driven recommendation agents. By analyzing a user's browsing and purchasing history—and often comparing it with similar user profiles—these agents suggest items they predict you'll want. This personalized experience can significantly increase sales, as customers discover products they might never have searched for on their own.

6.2 Chatbots and Customer Service Agents

Retailers and e-commerce platforms frequently deploy chatbots to provide immediate customer support. Advanced systems move beyond basic FAQs to natural language understanding. If someone asks, "Where's my order?" the agent can look up shipping data, verify the status, and respond in a conversational manner. While early chatbots were often criticized for clumsy interactions, newer versions use sophisticated language models capable of handling more nuanced dialogue.

6.3 Demand Forecasting and Dynamic Pricing

Sales can fluctuate based on season, trends, or even social media influence. AI agents capable of **demand forecasting** use historical sales data, weather predictions, and other external signals to predict spikes or dips in consumer interest. With those predictions, a business can adjust prices dynamically or allocate inventory to different regions. For example, if the AI detects a surge in demand for sunscreen in a region expecting a heat wave, it can prioritize shipping more units there. Dynamic pricing—raising or lowering prices based on demand—maximizes profits but can also draw scrutiny when prices jump too high during emergencies or critical events.

7. Broader Impacts on Work and Society

7.1 Changing Job Roles

As AI agents handle more tasks, humans may shift to new roles. For instance, a customer service representative might supervise multiple chatbot interactions, stepping in only when the conversation becomes too complex or emotionally charged. Similarly, factory workers might transition from manual labor to roles overseeing robotic operations, maintaining machines, or analyzing production data for continuous improvement.

Though the net effect on employment remains debated, it's clear that many jobs will evolve, emphasizing skills like critical thinking, creativity, emotional intelligence, and data literacy. Industries that adopt AI agents often see an uptick in demand for AI-savvy professionals who can design, monitor, or refine these systems.

7.2 Ethical and Regulatory Considerations

With AI agents deciding who qualifies for a loan, which job applicant moves forward, or what medical advice a patient receives, questions arise about bias, accountability, and transparency. Regulators in various countries are grappling with how to ensure these agents don't inadvertently discriminate or violate privacy. Some proposed regulations require "explainable" AI, meaning the systems must provide understandable rationales for their decisions.

In finance, for example, banks may have to demonstrate that automated loan approvals are not biased against certain demographics. In healthcare, a diagnostic AI must show adequate evidence that its recommendations are consistent with medical best practices. These demands for accountability drive research into "explainable AI" and highlight the need for strong oversight mechanisms.

7.3 Environmental Footprint

While AI agents can optimize processes to reduce energy and resource waste, training large-scale models and maintaining data centers also consumes significant electricity. Balancing efficiency gains against computational costs becomes an important consideration, especially for industries with large carbon footprints. Some organizations prioritize green data centers and model architectures that are more efficient—a trend likely to accelerate as sustainability becomes a focal point of corporate and public policy.

8. The Road Ahead: Opportunities and Challenges

As AI agents continue to expand into new areas, we can expect:

1. **Greater Personalization:** Products and services will be tailored more accurately to individual preferences, potentially increasing consumer satisfaction but also raising privacy concerns.
2. **Expanded Automation:** Industries from agriculture to education will discover new ways to integrate AI agents, automating repetitive tasks and even some tasks once considered uniquely human.
3. **Deeper Ethical Discussions:** The more decisions AI agents make, the more we'll question their fairness, transparency, and accountability.
4. **Emerging Business Models:** Entirely new services—like AI-powered subscription models for personalized healthcare—may become common, reshaping traditional sectors.

9. Key Takeaways

1. **Healthcare:** AI agents aid in diagnostics, personalized treatment, and ongoing patient monitoring, increasing efficiency and reducing error.
2. **Finance:** Fraud detection and algorithmic trading illustrate how real-time decision-making can reshape transactions, investment strategies, and personal finance management.

3. **Manufacturing:** From predictive maintenance to intelligent supply chains, AI agents cut costs, reduce downtime, and improve product quality.
4. **Transportation:** Autonomous vehicles and fleet management systems exemplify how AI can revolutionize logistics, though technical and regulatory barriers remain.
5. **Retail and E-commerce:** Personalized recommendations, dynamic pricing, and AI-powered customer service enhance both sales and user experience.

Whether you see these developments as thrilling or worrisome, they underscore the broad influence of AI agents across daily life. Recognizing their roles and potential pitfalls is key for consumers, workers, and policymakers alike.

10. Conclusion

From diagnosing diseases with greater accuracy to ensuring your online order arrives faster, AI agents are reshaping how business is conducted and how services are delivered. In many cases, these technologies operate invisibly—humming in the background as you shop, commute, or manage your finances. Their successes often stem from their ability to adapt to real-world challenges, learning from data and making decisions in real time.

Yet with great power comes a heightened responsibility to address issues of fairness, transparency, and the risk of job displacement. Industries that integrate AI agents must consider these societal impacts even as they pursue efficiency and profitability. Governments, too, are weighing how to regulate AI in ways that encourage innovation without sacrificing accountability.

In the following chapter, we'll shift our focus to the human–agent relationship. How do AI agents and people work together? What new skills will professionals need, and in which cases might automation fully replace human roles? By examining these questions, we'll get a clearer picture of the future of work—and how humans can thrive alongside increasingly capable AI agents.

6

The Human-Agent Team: Rethinking Work and Productivity

What happens when machines become coworkers rather than just tools? As AI agents grow more autonomous and widespread, they're not just handling repetitive tasks in the background; they're increasingly collaborating with people in dynamic, sophisticated ways. From virtual assistants in the workplace to intelligent software that helps leaders make strategic decisions, AI agents are reshaping our conception of labor and productivity. Rather than displacing humans wholesale, many argue that these agents can *augment* human capabilities and free us to focus on creativity, problem-solving, and interpersonal aspects of work. In this chapter, we'll explore how AI agents and humans combine their strengths, the skill shifts this demands, and the broader implications for industries and careers.

1. Collaboration vs. Replacement: A Complex Relationship

For decades, popular imagination has painted a future in which robots take over human jobs. While automation does indeed threaten certain roles, the reality is more nuanced. Many AI agents *collaborate* with people, enhancing what humans can do by taking on tasks that require speed, precision, or pattern detection at scale.

1.1 The Myth of Total Replacement

History offers numerous examples of technological advancement leading to changes in the job market. The Industrial Revolution automated textile production, for instance, displacing certain positions while creating new ones in factory oversight, design, and distribution. Computers replaced many clerical tasks but also generated a booming tech sector. AI agents follow a similar trajectory. While some roles may become obsolete or heavily transformed, many experts see a net shift rather than a net loss.

- **Displacement vs. Transformation:** A mail sorter might lose a job to AI-driven sorting machines, but that same organization may need more technicians to maintain and optimize the new technology.
- **Co-pilots, Not Replacements:** In fields like medicine, AI agents don't replace doctors; instead, they act as "co-pilots," quickly processing large datasets and offering insights or patterns that physicians incorporate into their expert judgment.

1.2 Where Machines Excel, and Where They Don't

AI agents shine at tasks involving repetitive operations, large-scale data analysis, and consistent application of rules. They rarely tire and can operate around the clock. Humans, on the other hand, excel in empathy, moral judgment, contextual understanding, and creative thinking. Industries that rely heavily on human interaction—such as counseling, relationship management, or creative arts—will likely rely on humans for the foreseeable future. Yet even in these areas, AI tools can assist by offering suggestions, gathering data, or automating routine chores.

2. New Skill Sets: Thriving in an AI-Augmented Workplace

As AI agents take on certain aspects of our work, humans have the opportunity to refocus on higher-level tasks. This shift drives demand for new skill sets that align with a more collaborative environment.

2.1 Data Literacy and Interpretation

When AI agents analyze data and present insights, someone must interpret those findings. Understanding data metrics, model limitations, and potential biases will be crucial to making informed decisions. Whether you're a marketer examining customer analytics or a policy officer reviewing crime statistics, the ability to **question** and **contextualize** an AI's results becomes part of modern professional competence.

- **Asking the Right Questions:** When an AI flags a potential trend (e.g., "Sales might dip in the Midwest next quarter"), managers who can probe deeper—asking about underlying assumptions or the data used—are better equipped to turn these insights into actionable strategies.

- **Spotting Biases:** If an AI recruiting tool has been trained on a dataset lacking demographic diversity, the system may inadvertently filter out qualified applicants from underrepresented groups. Recognizing such pitfalls requires people who understand both the AI's methods and broader societal context.

2.2 Creativity and Critical Thinking

As machines handle routine tasks, the unique human ability to brainstorm, innovate, and evaluate complex scenarios becomes even more valuable. AI might propose multiple solutions to a problem—say, optimizing a delivery route—but it's the human who weighs the trade-offs, such as community impact or environmental considerations, that go beyond raw efficiency metrics.

- **Adaptive Problem-Solving:** Roles that demand thinking "outside the box" will rise in significance. For example, a logistics manager might integrate an AI's suggestions for truck routing with local knowledge (roadwork, community events) and shift strategies on the fly.
- **Strategic Foresight:** AI can simulate many "what if" scenarios, but humans still excel at shaping the overarching vision—connecting disparate ideas, building consensus among stakeholders, and adapting strategies to evolving cultural or market conditions.

2.3 Emotional and Social Intelligence

Much of professional life hinges on empathy, negotiation, and relationship-building. AI may help identify potential partners or quantify customer feedback, but forging genuine connections often requires the subtleties of human interaction.

- **Leadership and Team Coordination:** Motivating a team, understanding interpersonal dynamics, and making ethical decisions remain predominantly human strengths. Leaders skilled at blending AI-driven data with emotional intelligence can nurture stronger organizations.
- **Customer Service at Higher Levels:** While a chatbot can handle routine questions, escalations or sensitive issues typically require a human touch. Professionals adept at advanced troubleshooting and emotional support will remain essential.

3. Enhanced Productivity: Unlocking Human Potential

One of the major advantages of the human–agent partnership is the possibility of boosting overall productivity by combining the speed and consistency of machines with human ingenuity and empathy.

3.1 Automating the Drudgery

Many employees spend a portion of their day doing mundane tasks—data entry, scheduling, or repetitive calculations. AI agents can automate these chores, freeing people for tasks that better leverage human strengths.

- **Administrative Relief:** Digital assistants can schedule meetings, respond to basic emails, and organize files, allowing professionals to focus on strategic work.
- **Reduced Errors:** Systems that automate repetitive tasks are less prone to human error (like typos or miscalculations), increasing overall accuracy and potentially saving money.

3.2 Real-Time Decision Support

In fields like finance or emergency response, the ability to make swift, data-informed decisions can be critical. AI agents can filter through mountains of information—such as market fluctuations or real-time weather updates—so that humans can make informed choices quickly.

- **Financial Trading:** Traders can rely on AI to alert them about subtle market shifts, then inject their own market knowledge or risk tolerance when executing trades.
- **Disaster Management:** In wildfire situations, AI drones might scan the area for fire spread patterns, relaying data to human teams who then decide when to evacuate neighborhoods or deploy additional resources.

3.3 Creativity Amplification

Tools powered by AI increasingly offer suggestions for improving writing, designing graphics, composing music, or coding software. Instead of viewing these suggestions as competition, many professionals see them as inspiration—sparking new ideas and refining initial concepts more quickly.

- **Writing and Design:** An AI text-generation tool might provide a draft for an ad campaign, which a human copywriter then personalizes and polishes.
- **Software Development:** "Pair programming" with an AI agent can accelerate code completion and reduce bugs by catching errors or suggesting efficient algorithms on the fly.

4. Sector Spotlights: Human-Agent Teams in Different Industries

Let's consider specific examples of how human–agent teaming looks in various fields:

4.1 Healthcare Collaboration

Physicians increasingly rely on AI diagnostic tools to spot anomalies in medical images or suggest possible treatments. While an AI might highlight potential tumors more effectively than a single human eye, the doctor remains responsible for integrating these findings into a comprehensive patient plan that accounts for factors like family history, patient preferences, and overall well-being.

This synergy can lead to faster and more accurate diagnoses, but it also requires physicians trained in interpreting AI suggestions and challenging the technology when something doesn't align with clinical judgment. At the same time, healthcare professionals can spend more time on patient interaction, addressing emotional and psychological needs.

4.2 Construction and Engineering

BIM (Building Information Modeling) software with AI capabilities can design or optimize building plans, proposing structural solutions that meet safety standards and cost constraints. Engineers then refine these plans, factoring in local climate, aesthetic preferences, and cultural or historical considerations.

On the construction site, AI-powered robots might handle repetitive tasks like bricklaying or material transport, allowing skilled workers to focus on complex activities that require on-the-spot problem-solving—like adapting to unexpected ground conditions or integrating last-minute architectural changes.

4.3 Journalism and Media

Journalists increasingly use AI agents to sift through massive datasets—financial reports, legal documents, or social media feeds—unearthing trends or anomalies that could inspire investigative stories. The AI can highlight suspicious patterns in political donations, for example, but it's the journalist's job to investigate, verify sources, and craft a narrative that resonates with readers.

In real-time coverage (e.g., breaking news or sports), AI chatbots might produce instantaneous short updates, while human editors provide context, depth, and emotional weight. This dynamic division of labor can allow news organizations to cover more ground in a shorter timeframe without losing the human voice that connects with audiences.

5. Overcoming Challenges in Human-Agent Collaboration

While the benefits of teaming humans with AI agents are clear, several challenges can hinder smooth integration.

5.1 Trust and Transparency

When an AI agent makes a recommendation—like denying a loan application or highlighting a suspect in a crime case—how can humans trust that decision? Ensuring that AI processes are transparent and understandable remains a major challenge. Workers and consumers need confidence that AI-driven decisions are fair, accurate, and explainable.

- **Explainable AI:** Researchers are developing methods for AI systems to "show their work," revealing key factors behind a decision. This helps users trust the system's outputs and identify potential errors.
- **Regulations and Guidelines:** Governments and professional bodies increasingly demand that AI be auditable, especially in high-stakes sectors such as finance, healthcare, and law enforcement.

5.2 Role Definition and Skill Gaps

Integrating AI agents can create confusion over who's responsible for certain tasks—or who gets credit for a successful project. Clearly defining roles, responsibilities, and escalations (when to involve a human supervisor) avoids misunderstandings.

- **New Training Programs:** Companies adopting AI at scale

often need to reskill employees, teaching them how to work effectively alongside intelligent systems—interpreting outputs, validating suggestions, and knowing the boundaries of the technology.

- **Cross-Functional Teams:** AI development is no longer just the domain of software engineers. Ethicists, data analysts, and subject-matter experts all play roles in ensuring a system meets its intended goals and values.

5.3 Resistance to Change

Some employees may view AI as a threat, potentially leading to a lack of cooperation or even sabotage. Transparency around how AI will impact roles—alongside opportunities for upskilling—can alleviate fears. Building a workplace culture that frames AI as a tool for empowerment rather than replacement encourages adoption.

- **Communication and Stakeholder Engagement:** Proactive communication from leadership—sharing success stories, addressing concerns openly—can help diffuse anxiety.
- **Pilot Programs and Incremental Adoption:** Gradually introducing AI in non-critical processes allows teams to acclimate and build trust before the technology expands to core operations.

6. The Bigger Picture: Toward a New Productivity Paradigm

Many economists and futurists argue that advanced AI will herald a new era of productivity, akin to the shifts brought about by electricity or the personal computer. Instead of focusing on how many hours we log doing rote tasks, the emphasis could shift to **value creation**—novel ideas, meaningful relationships, and quality of life improvements.

6.1 Rethinking "Work"

If AI agents handle mundane chores, the structure of work itself might shift. Some theorize we could move toward shorter workweeks as "productivity traps"—like busywork—diminish. Others see people spending more time on tasks that require social and creative skills. Although this outcome is not guaranteed, it raises important questions about how societies reward labor and define success.

6.2 Changing Business Models

From manufacturing to consulting, businesses that successfully integrate human-agent teams may enjoy a competitive edge. They can make decisions faster, innovate more effectively, and adapt to market changes more fluidly. In turn, this might prompt new forms of organizational design—less hierarchical, more project-based, with AI as a core collaborator in decision-making processes.

6.3 Global Implications

Developing countries with rapidly growing industries could use AI to leapfrog certain stages of industrialization, automating tasks that require large, unskilled labor forces in traditional models. This shift has pros and cons—it could accelerate economic development, but it might also reduce job opportunities. International bodies and nonprofits are beginning to explore how AI can be used responsibly to foster inclusive growth across diverse economies.

7. Key Takeaways

1. **Collaboration vs. Replacement:** While AI agents can automate some tasks entirely, many roles shift rather than vanish, becoming more collaborative and strategically oriented.
2. **Evolving Skill Sets:** Data literacy, creativity, critical thinking, and emotional intelligence grow in importance as AI handles routine or repetitive work.
3. **Enhanced Productivity:** Automation of mundane tasks and real-time decision support can significantly boost efficiency, freeing people for higher-level problem-solving.
4. **Challenges:** Building trust in AI decisions, defining new roles, and overcoming resistance are critical for successful integration.
5. **Future of Work:** AI agents could redefine the meaning of "work," potentially changing job structures, economic models, and global development patterns.

8. Conclusion

The partnership between humans and AI agents is transforming how we think about productivity, collaboration, and the nature of work itself. Far from a one-sided replacement scenario, the reality is an evolving tapestry of tasks—some optimally performed by AI, others still best suited to human intuition, creativity, and empathy. For many organizations and individuals, the challenge lies in orchestrating this interplay effectively: ensuring that AI agents have the data and oversight they need, while humans stay engaged and informed enough to guide strategic decisions and ethical considerations.

In the next chapter, we'll expand on the broader societal and ethical implications of these trends—considering not just how human-agent teams can achieve remarkable productivity gains, but also how potential pitfalls, biases, and disruptive effects on labor markets must be managed responsibly. By looking at our collective future, we can better understand how to harness the promise of AI agents in ways that benefit everyone.

7

Ethical Frameworks and Responsible AI Agents

Amid the excitement about AI's potential to revolutionize work and society, a pressing question looms: *How do we ensure that AI agents act responsibly?* As systems become more autonomous, the consequences of their decisions grow more significant—sometimes even life-altering. Whether diagnosing patients, approving loans, or guiding self-driving vehicles, AI agents are entrusted with roles that demand a high level of ethical scrutiny. This chapter unpacks the core ethical considerations associated with AI agents, from bias and accountability to privacy and security. We'll explore the frameworks that researchers, companies, and governments are developing to guide AI agents toward more equitable and transparent outcomes, and we'll consider how individuals and communities can play a role in shaping responsible AI practices.

1. The Challenge of Ethical AI

When you think of ethics, you might picture a human weighing moral principles before making a decision. But an AI agent, driven by algorithms and data, lacks intrinsic moral awareness. It relies on mathematical functions, optimization goals, and historical patterns learned from training sets. This dependence on data and code can make AI agents vulnerable to certain pitfalls:

1. **Bias:** If the data reflects societal prejudices, the AI may perpetuate or even amplify them.
2. **Opacity:** Complex models, particularly deep neural networks, can be "black boxes," making it difficult to understand how they arrive at decisions.
3. **Accountability:** If an AI agent makes a harmful decision, it's unclear who is ultimately responsible—the developer, the user, the organization that deployed it?
4. **Security:** As AI agents become interconnected with critical infrastructure, their vulnerabilities become new avenues for cyberattacks or malicious manipulation.

Addressing these challenges requires a combination of technological solutions, policy frameworks, and cultural awareness. The stakes are high, because AI agents increasingly influence everything from personal credit scores to national security decisions.

2. Bias and Fairness

2.1 How Bias Creeps In

Bias can infiltrate AI systems in several ways. The most common is **biased data**. For example, suppose an AI recruiting tool is trained primarily on résumés from one demographic group. It might learn patterns that favor that group, inadvertently penalizing candidates who don't match those historical trends. Another source of bias is **algorithmic design**, where certain variables or weights skew results in ways the designers didn't anticipate.

Biases in AI systems matter because they can manifest at scale, impacting large groups of people. For instance, a mortgage-lending AI might systematically offer higher interest rates to certain zip codes if historical data reflects long-standing economic disparities. Even if no human actively intends to discriminate, the AI's reliance on flawed patterns can lead to real-world injustices.

2.2 Strategies to Mitigate Bias

1. **Diverse and Representative Datasets:** Ensuring that training data encompasses different backgrounds, geographies, and perspectives helps the AI "see" a broader range of human experiences.
2. **Algorithmic Audits:** Regular reviews can identify where the model is misclassifying or producing skewed outcomes. Organizations can then retrain or refine the model to correct these tendencies.
3. **Fairness Metrics:** Researchers develop mathematical measures (e.g., equalized odds, demographic parity) that quantify how equitable an AI's decisions are across differ-

ent groups.

4. **Human Oversight:** In high-stakes domains, human experts can review the AI's most impactful decisions, especially when anomalies appear.

3. Transparency and Explainability

3.1 The "Black Box" Problem

Neural networks and other complex algorithms often process information in ways that defy easy explanation. A self-driving car might "decide" to change lanes after considering thousands of subtle features—like sensor inputs, speed limits, or predicted behaviors of nearby vehicles. If the car malfunctions, it's challenging to pinpoint which factor or combination of factors led to the error.

This opacity raises concerns in sectors like healthcare, where doctors and patients want to know *why* an AI recommended a particular treatment, or in finance, where regulators demand clarity on loan approvals or rejections. When decisions feel unexplainable, trust in AI systems erodes.

3.2 Approaches to Explainable AI

1. **Feature Attribution Tools:** Techniques such as saliency maps or SHAP (SHapley Additive exPlanations) attempt to highlight which inputs most influenced the AI's output.
2. **Interpretable Models:** Instead of using the largest, deepest networks, some developers opt for simpler, more transparent algorithms like decision trees. While this might sacrifice some accuracy in complex tasks, it can

greatly enhance clarity and trust.

3. **Surrogate Models:** In cases where a high-performing black-box model is necessary, a simpler "surrogate" model can approximate its behavior. This surrogate is easier to interpret and can give insights into how the primary system operates—though it's still an approximation.
4. **Regulatory Incentives:** Some jurisdictions are pushing for laws that mandate a certain level of explainability for AI systems affecting consumers, particularly around credit, employment, or healthcare decisions.

4. Accountability: Who Bears the Blame?

As AI agents become more autonomous, the question of *responsibility* looms large. Imagine a self-driving car swerving incorrectly and causing an accident, or an AI medical tool overlooking a critical symptom. Who should be held liable?

4.1 Shared Responsibility

In many cases, responsibility may be shared among several stakeholders:

- **Developers and Designers:** Those who built and trained the AI could be held accountable if design flaws or poor testing protocols contributed to harmful outcomes.
- **Organizations Deploying the AI:** A hospital, bank, or city government that chooses to use an AI system has a duty to ensure its safe and appropriate use.
- **End Users:** If human operators are meant to supervise the

AI and intervene in emergencies, their vigilance (or lack thereof) might factor into accountability.

4.2 Emerging Legal Frameworks

Legal systems worldwide are grappling with how to codify AI accountability. Some proposed frameworks involve:

- **Strict Liability for High-Risk AI:** In especially risky domains—like autonomous vehicles or medical devices—manufacturers or operators could be held strictly liable if their AI system causes harm, regardless of fault.
- **No-Fault Compensation Funds:** An alternative is to establish compensation schemes that assist victims without protracted legal battles to prove negligence.
- **Regulatory Sandboxes:** Governments allow controlled testing of AI systems, gathering data on potential failures and clarifying liability before widespread deployment.

Accountability provisions aren't just punitive; they also incentivize safer, more transparent design. When developers know they could face legal consequences, they're more likely to follow robust testing and ethical guidelines.

5. Security and Privacy: Shielding AI from Malicious Use

5.1 Security Threats

As AI agents become integral to critical infrastructure—power grids, transportation systems, financial networks—they present tempting targets for cybercriminals or hostile actors.

An attacker who compromises an AI agent might manipulate its decisions, leading to anything from financial fraud to sabotage of public utilities.

Additionally, "adversarial attacks" exploit the weaknesses of machine learning algorithms. In one famous example, researchers showed that by adding subtle noise patterns to street signs, they could trick an AI into misreading a Stop sign as a Speed Limit sign, potentially causing catastrophic results for self-driving cars.

5.2 Protecting AI Systems

1. **Robust Training Methods:** Developers can train AI models on adversarial examples—specially crafted data that tests the system's resilience to tampering. This helps models learn to recognize and ignore deceptive inputs.
2. **Secure Data Pipelines:** Ensuring the integrity and encryption of data at every stage—from collection to model training to deployment—minimizes the risk of malicious alterations.
3. **Continuous Monitoring:** Organizations that rely on AI for mission-critical tasks often maintain 24/7 monitoring, ready to shut down or override systems showing anomalous behavior.
4. **Ethical Hacking and Red Teams:** Some companies employ experts who attempt to break or deceive AI systems, identifying weaknesses before real adversaries do.

5.3 Privacy Concerns

Beyond security, AI agents raise privacy questions because they often rely on personal data—be it financial history, health records, or location tracking. If people fear misuse or unauthorized sharing of their data, trust in AI systems deteriorates. Regulatory frameworks like Europe's General Data Protection Regulation (GDPR) and California's Consumer Privacy Act (CCPA) set stringent guidelines on data usage, ensuring individuals have some control over how their information is collected and processed.

6. Guidelines and Frameworks for Responsible AI

6.1 Industry Efforts

Many tech giants and research institutions have published ethical guidelines to steer AI development:

- **Google's AI Principles:** Focused on social benefit, avoidance of bias, and accountability.
- **IBM's Everyday Ethics for AI:** Emphasizes transparency, privacy, and inclusivity.
- **Microsoft's Responsible AI Principles:** Includes fairness, reliability and safety, privacy and security, inclusiveness, transparency, and accountability.

While these statements mark a step toward self-regulation, critics argue that without binding enforcement, these guidelines can be more public relations than substance. Nonetheless, they set a precedent for internal oversight and signal the industry's recognition of ethical priorities.

6.2 Government and International Initiatives

Governments worldwide are also shaping AI regulations. The European Union (EU) has proposed the **Artificial Intelligence Act**, which categorizes AI applications based on risk (from minimal to unacceptable) and sets requirements accordingly. International bodies like the OECD have put forth *Principles on AI*, urging member nations to adopt values of human-centeredness, robustness, and accountability in AI deployment.

In addition, organizations such as UNESCO have adopted AI ethics recommendations that encourage cross-cultural dialogue and emphasize human rights, ensuring technology respects diverse perspectives and traditions.

6.3 Independent Oversight

Some experts propose creating independent agencies or boards with the power to audit AI systems and mandate improvements. For instance, a national or global AI oversight committee could investigate allegations of bias, examine critical algorithms for safety, and impose penalties for violations—similar to how financial regulators oversee banking.

7. Ethical Decision-Making Within Organizations

7.1 Building an Ethical Culture

Ethics doesn't emerge solely from guidelines—it's reinforced by an organization's culture. Companies that encourage employees to flag ethical concerns, even if it slows down a product launch, are more likely to avoid major pitfalls. This "speak-up" culture might involve:

- **Ethics Training:** Ensuring all employees, from data scientists to marketing staff, understand potential biases, privacy risks, and fairness obligations.
- **Ethics Committees or Boards:** Groups that review AI projects for alignment with the company's ethical guidelines before deployment.
- **Internal Transparency:** Open communication about the AI tools used, their limitations, and the measures taken to mitigate risks.

7.2 Responsible Design Process

Engineers and product managers can incorporate ethical considerations at each step of development:

1. **Define Goals Carefully:** Rather than solely optimizing for profit or efficiency, incorporate metrics like fairness, privacy preservation, or user well-being.
2. **Continuous Testing:** An AI system's performance can degrade or shift over time if the real-world environment differs from the training scenario. Regular checks help detect bias drift or unintended consequences.
3. **Human in the Loop:** For high-stakes decisions—medical

diagnoses, loan approvals—organizations can require a human reviewer to approve the AI's recommendation, at least until the system demonstrates consistent reliability.

8. The Role of the Public

While much of the responsibility for ethical AI rests on developers, companies, and governments, everyday people also play a part. **Consumer pressure**—through purchasing decisions or public campaigns—can push companies to adopt more rigorous standards. **Voter engagement** shapes how politicians address AI regulation. And **community advocacy** can highlight how certain technologies (like facial recognition in public spaces) might threaten civil liberties.

By staying informed, asking critical questions about how AI systems collect data, and advocating for transparency, citizens help shape the ethical contours of AI. Ultimately, an informed, engaged public is a powerful force in steering technology toward societal good.

9. Toward a More Equitable AI Future

Ensuring AI agents are fair, transparent, and accountable is not just a moral imperative—it's essential for maintaining public trust and maximizing the technology's potential for positive impact. An AI system that consistently discriminates or hides its logic will eventually erode confidence, slowing innovation as users back away. By contrast, robust ethical frameworks foster a collaborative ecosystem where humans and AI can thrive together.

9.1 Potential Benefits of Ethical AI

- **Wider Adoption:** Ethical systems are more likely to be embraced in sensitive domains like healthcare, finance, and public policy.
- **Global Cooperation:** Shared ethical standards can reduce tension between regions or nations worried about AI misuse, paving the way for collaborative research and problem-solving.
- **Innovation with Integrity:** When developers and businesses operate with strong ethical guardrails, they can explore cutting-edge ideas without sacrificing human rights or social values.

9.2 The Ongoing Conversation

Ethical AI is not a fixed endpoint but a continuous process of adaptation. As technology evolves—from new deep learning architectures to multi-agent systems that might collectively behave in unforeseen ways—our ethical standards and methods of oversight must evolve with it. Ongoing dialogue among researchers, policymakers, developers, ethicists, and the public ensures that we keep refining what "responsible AI" means in practice.

10. Key Takeaways

1. **Bias and Fairness:** AI agents can perpetuate societal prejudices if trained on biased data or poorly designed algorithms, highlighting the need for careful audits and diverse datasets.

2. **Transparency and Explainability:** Complex "black box" systems undermine trust; explainable AI is crucial for high-stakes decisions.
3. **Accountability:** As AI agents become more autonomous, responsibility for errors can be shared among developers, deploying organizations, and end users—underscoring the need for clear legal frameworks.
4. **Security and Privacy:** Robust safeguards are essential to prevent adversarial attacks and protect personal data, maintaining trust in AI-driven services.
5. **Ethical Guidelines and Oversight:** Industry principles, government regulations, and organizational cultures all influence how AI is developed and deployed, but these must be backed by tangible enforcement and transparent processes.
6. **Public Engagement:** Informed consumers, voters, and community advocates play a pivotal role in demanding and shaping ethical AI policies.

11. Conclusion

As AI agents integrate deeper into daily life—scanning medical scans, approving loans, recommending prison sentences, or guiding self-driving vehicles—questions of ethics, fairness, and accountability become increasingly urgent. The solutions are multifaceted: better data practices, technical innovations in explainability, robust legal standards, and a culture of responsibility within organizations. Equally vital is the active participation of the public, whose concerns and aspirations must guide the AI revolution toward inclusive and equitable outcomes.

In the chapters to come, we'll explore how these ethical frameworks interact with society at large, including the potential for AI agents to disrupt labor markets, reshape economic power structures, and influence global policymaking. By delving deeper into these socio-economic dimensions, we'll gain a more holistic view of how to steer AI's rapid advancement in ways that respect human dignity and mutual well-being.

8

Societal Impact and Disruption

From chatbots in our mobile apps to autonomous delivery drones on city streets, AI agents are rapidly redefining how we work, communicate, and solve problems. As these agents become more integrated into day-to-day life, they inevitably spark significant shifts across economies, labor markets, cultural norms, and governance structures. While their benefits can be immense—fueling innovation, productivity, and even new forms of creativity—the accompanying disruptions pose real challenges. In this chapter, we examine how AI agents are influencing society at large, highlighting both positive outcomes and areas of concern that demand our attention.

1. A New Economic Landscape

1.1 Growth and Productivity Gains

Historically, major technological breakthroughs—like the steam engine or the internet—have propelled economic growth. AI agents represent a similarly transformative wave. By automating routine tasks, analyzing data at lightning speed, and operating around the clock, these intelligent systems can radically boost efficiency. Manufacturers that use AI-driven robotics can produce more goods in less time and at lower cost. Service-oriented companies benefit from automated customer support bots, which handle basic inquiries and free human agents to solve more complex problems. The cumulative effect is an overall rise in productivity that can, at least in theory, generate economic growth and wealth.

1.2 Rising Inequalities

Yet productivity gains don't automatically translate into broad-based prosperity. A key concern is whether AI-driven efficiency primarily benefits large companies and highly skilled workers, leaving others behind. For instance, industries that automate extensively may shrink their workforce. Meanwhile, employees with the expertise to develop, implement, and maintain AI systems may command higher wages, exacerbating income disparities. This "winner-take-all" dynamic could widen existing gaps between socioeconomic classes, regions, and even entire countries—especially if wealth concentrates among companies and individuals who already possess capital and technical know-how.

1.3 New Business Models

On a brighter note, AI agents also enable novel business models that democratize certain opportunities. For example, small businesses can outsource back-office tasks to AI-driven software-as-a-service platforms, saving time and costs that previously required hiring full-time staff. Freelancers can market themselves globally and leverage AI-driven productivity tools to punch above their weight. Startups can scale faster by combining minimal human staff with AI agents that handle marketing, scheduling, or customer analytics. These developments can, in some cases, distribute the benefits of AI more widely—provided entrepreneurs, policymakers, and the public are ready to embrace them.

2. The Great Reallocation: Jobs and Skills

2.1 Automation and Displacement

Perhaps the most immediate societal impact of AI agents is the disruption of labor markets. Automation is nothing new—think of how mechanical looms replaced manual textile workers in the 19th century—but AI pushes this trend further. Jobs involving repetitive or predictable tasks, such as entry-level data processing or simple customer support, face significant risk of automation. Even roles once viewed as requiring deep expertise—like medical image analysis—are being augmented (if not fully replaced) by AI agents. As we've seen in earlier chapters, in many scenarios these agents work alongside humans, but the trajectory can still shift job requirements drastically.

2.2 Emerging Occupations

On the flipside, AI agents also create new occupations. Demand for data scientists, machine learning engineers, AI ethicists, and "explainability experts" is growing. Beyond these technical roles, industries need professionals who can interpret AI-driven insights in contexts like healthcare, law, education, and government policy. There's an increasing need for "bridge" roles—people who combine domain expertise (e.g., insurance or agriculture) with AI know-how to oversee the integration of intelligent systems responsibly. This pivot parallels the early internet era, when web designers and IT specialists became essential to nearly every business.

2.3 Re-Skilling and Education

If the workforce is to adapt, education systems must pivot to equip students and mid-career workers with new skills. Traditional rote learning becomes less relevant when machines can master memorization tasks instantly. Instead, curricula should emphasize critical thinking, creativity, emotional intelligence, and digital literacy. These skills are harder to automate and complement AI-driven insights. Governments and corporations alike face mounting pressure to invest in re-skilling and up-skilling programs, lest entire segments of the workforce be left behind in the AI-driven economy.

3. Policy, Regulation, and Governance

3.1 The Role of Governments

With AI agents influencing job markets, consumer choices, and even national security, governments have a growing stake in AI regulation. As we explored in the previous chapter on ethics, public policies around bias, transparency, and accountability are critical. But beyond these ethical frameworks, policymakers must also address economic and social consequences. For instance, should governments provide universal basic income (UBI) if automation displaces large numbers of workers? How should antitrust laws evolve to prevent AI-driven monopolies? These questions have no simple answers, but they underscore the need for proactive governance.

3.2 Public Infrastructure and Access

AI capabilities depend heavily on robust digital infrastructure—everything from high-speed internet to cloud computing services. Regions lacking this infrastructure risk falling further behind. Governments could invest in public data centers or encourage private sector collaboration to bridge connectivity gaps. Additionally, they may need to set standards for data sharing and open-source AI tools, ensuring smaller players and developing countries can benefit from AI breakthroughs, not just those with deep pockets.

3.3 International Cooperation and Competition

AI doesn't respect national borders. Multinational tech companies deploy AI-driven products globally, while data flows freely across the internet. Consequently, international bodies like the European Union (EU) and the United Nations (UN) are exploring coordinated AI strategies. At the same time, countries may view AI as a competitive advantage, racing to develop advanced military drones or commercial platforms. Striking a balance between collaboration (to tackle shared ethical or environmental concerns) and competition (to spur innovation) is one of the defining policy challenges of our time.

4. Cultural and Social Effects

4.1 Shifts in Identity and Self-Worth

For many, careers and work are deeply tied to personal identity and social status. As AI agents reshape the labor market, some individuals may feel a loss of purpose when their profession is automated or radically changed. Conversely, those who adapt and find new vocations may discover fresh opportunities for personal growth. Societies might need to redefine how they value work and leisure, potentially recognizing caregiving or creative pursuits more formally as AI takes over routine tasks.

4.2 Community and Social Interactions

Human–machine interactions are becoming part of everyday life, influencing how we interact with one another. Think about how social media algorithms recommend friends or how a dating app's AI suggests potential partners. AI agents subtly guide many of our social interactions—a phenomenon sometimes called the "algorithmic curation" of our social sphere. This can foster connections between like-minded people, but it can also create "filter bubbles," making us less exposed to diverse viewpoints. Communities may need to proactively ensure that technology promotes social cohesion rather than splintering it.

4.3 Mental Health Implications

While AI agents can improve mental health outcomes—providing basic therapy chats or connecting individuals to resources—they may also inadvertently cause stress or isolation. Increased screen time, potential job insecurity, and privacy concerns can exacerbate anxiety. Well-designed AI interventions could mitigate these risks by offering mental health support at scale, but policymakers, designers, and healthcare professionals need to stay vigilant about the quality and ethical deployment of these tools.

5. AI in Public Discourse: Democracy and Misinformation

5.1 Misinformation and Echo Chambers

AI-driven bots can fabricate articles, generate misleading social media posts, or amplify divisive content—often faster than human fact-checkers can respond. As these agents become more sophisticated, it gets harder for average citizens to distinguish genuine information from manipulative or fake content. The risk is that entire communities could be swayed by orchestrated AI campaigns, undermining trust in media and institutions.

5.2 Impact on Democratic Processes

Election campaigns increasingly employ AI-driven strategies to micro-target voters with personalized messages. While this can help politicians tailor their platforms more closely to constituent concerns, it also raises concerns about manipulation and the lack of transparency around how ads and political content are delivered. In the worst case, AI-fueled misinformation could skew electoral outcomes or delegitimize democratic institutions.

5.3 Potential Solutions

Efforts to curb AI-driven misinformation include better content moderation tools, stricter social media policies, and collaborations between tech firms and fact-checking organizations. However, these solutions themselves can raise ethical dilemmas about censorship and free speech. Balancing the need for accurate information with the principles of open discourse remains a major societal challenge.

6. Education and Lifelong Learning

6.1 Rethinking Curricula

As AI agents automate certain skill-based tasks, educational systems must adapt. Schools that still prioritize rote memorization risk leaving students unprepared for an era where machine-based analytics and data processing are ubiquitous. Instead, educators may emphasize problem-solving, critical thinking, collaboration, and ethical reasoning—areas in which human abilities still surpass AI. A project-based learning approach, integrating technology hands-on from an early age, could empower future generations to navigate AI-rich environments confidently.

6.2 Lifelong Learning

With the rapid pace of technological change, people may need to continually update their skill sets. AI-driven training platforms can help by personalizing learning modules for each individual's pace and interests. This model of "lifelong learning" might become the new normal, replacing the old notion that a single phase of formal education prepares you for a decades-long career. Governments and businesses can support these shifts by funding accessible training programs and incentivizing ongoing professional development.

6.3 Bridging the Digital Divide

Not everyone has equal access to advanced learning tools or stable internet connections. Rural communities, lower-income groups, and developing nations often lag behind in digital infrastructure, creating a global AI "haves vs. have-nots." Addressing this divide is critical if society wants AI-driven opportunities—like online education, remote work, or telemedicine—to be truly inclusive. Partnerships among governments, NGOs, and tech companies could provide hardware, subsidized connectivity, and localized training to narrow these gaps.

7. Global Impact: Collaboration and Uneven Development

7.1 Potential for Worldwide Benefits

AI agents can address pressing global challenges: analyzing climate data to predict natural disasters, optimizing agricultural practices for food security, or allocating healthcare resources during pandemics. When used cooperatively, AI can transcend borders and expedite solutions that benefit humanity as a whole. By pooling data and computational power internationally, researchers can tackle shared problems—like infectious disease outbreaks or environmental crises—more effectively than any single country acting alone.

7.2 Risk of Unequal Adoption

However, countries with substantial AI research budgets and tech infrastructure—primarily in North America, Europe, and East Asia—tend to lead innovations. Developing nations, meanwhile, risk becoming consumers of AI technology rather than co-creators. This asymmetry can perpetuate dependency and hinder local industries from building their own AI expertise. The resulting "AI gap" may parallel existing economic disparities, raising ethical questions about how to ensure fair global participation in AI development and usage.

7.3 Multi-Stakeholder Approaches

International alliances, such as cross-border partnerships and open-source AI research communities, can help distribute knowledge more evenly. Some tech companies open their AI frameworks to the public, enabling smaller startups or researchers in developing countries to build on existing tools without paying exorbitant licensing fees. Likewise, philanthropic initiatives can fund AI centers of excellence in underserved regions, fostering a more balanced global AI ecosystem.

8. Conclusion

AI agents aren't just technological marvels; they're powerful catalysts for social, economic, and cultural change. Their capacity to transform industries and democratize certain processes comes with real risks: job displacement, widening inequalities, misinformation, and potential destabilization of democratic norms. Yet the same technology can also deliver unprecedented efficiencies, open new career paths, advance global collaboration, and address humanitarian crises.

Society's collective response will shape whether AI agents become forces for equitable prosperity or engines of division and disenfranchisement. Policymakers can craft legislation that safeguards fairness and accountability, educators can prepare the workforce for a rapidly evolving economy, and businesses can implement AI ethically while fostering inclusivity. Meanwhile, everyday citizens—acting as informed consumers, voters, and community advocates—play a vital role in pushing AI development toward transparency and social good.

In the next chapter, we'll explore the cutting edge of AI research—delving deeper into how **reinforcement learning** and **multi-agent collaboration** might reshape not just industries but also the very nature of intelligence itself. By understanding these frontiers, we can better anticipate new disruptions on the horizon and engage proactively in shaping a future where AI agents work in harmony with human values.

9

The Next Frontiers: Reinforcement Learning and Multi-Agent Collaboration

Over the past chapters, we've explored how AI agents have evolved, the diverse roles they play in modern industries, and how their use is reshaping societies. Now, we turn to some of the most cutting-edge areas in AI research: **reinforcement learning (RL)** and **multi-agent collaboration**. These dynamic fields push the boundaries of what AI can do, moving beyond single-task solutions toward sophisticated systems capable of complex decision-making, teamwork, and even emergent forms of intelligence. In this chapter, we'll unpack these concepts in plain language—illuminating their core ideas, real-world applications, and the potential they hold for transforming everything from disaster relief to economics.

1. Why Reinforcement Learning Matters

Reinforcement learning (RL) is an approach to AI that mimics how humans and animals learn through trial and error. In RL, an *agent* interacts with an *environment*, receiving *rewards* (positive or negative) based on its actions. Over time, the agent refines its strategy (or *policy*) to maximize cumulative rewards. Imagine training a dog: when it performs a trick correctly, it gets a treat (reward); when it does something wrong, it gets no treat (or a gentle correction). RL algorithms operate on a similar principle—just in a digital space.

1.1 Moving Beyond Static Data

Traditional supervised learning relies on labeled data. You feed the algorithm thousands of examples—images of cats and dogs, for instance—and it learns to distinguish between them. But in many real-world settings, you can't rely on a static dataset. Consider self-driving cars: they must navigate unpredictable roads, reacting to changing traffic patterns, weather conditions, and pedestrian behavior.

Reinforcement learning offers a solution by allowing agents to learn on the fly. Instead of being explicitly told "this is right" or "this is wrong," an RL agent receives a scalar reward—perhaps a slight increase for staying in its lane safely, or a penalty for veering too close to another car. By experimenting and observing the outcomes, the agent evolves its driving strategy.

1.2 Key Concepts in Reinforcement Learning

1. **State:** A representation of the current situation (e.g., car location, speed, road layout).
2. **Action:** A move the agent can make (e.g., turn left, accelerate, brake).
3. **Reward:** A numerical signal indicating how good or bad

the outcome of an action was (e.g., +1 for a safe move, -10 for a collision).

4. **Policy:** The agent's strategy—a mapping from states to actions that it refines over time.

Common algorithms—like Q-learning or policy gradients—help the agent update its policy to achieve higher rewards.

2. RL in Action: From Games to Real-World Applications

2.1 High-Profile Successes

Reinforcement learning first captured headlines through **game-playing agents**. Google DeepMind's AlphaGo famously defeated top-ranked human players in the board game Go, a game that was once thought too complex for machines to master. Even more impressively, AlphaZero learned to excel at Go, chess, and shogi from scratch—playing against itself millions of times and refining its policy without human intervention.

In video games, RL agents have reached or surpassed human-level performance in classics like Atari Breakout and more complex arenas like StarCraft II. These achievements highlight the adaptability of RL: by simulating environments at speed, agents can gather immense experience in a fraction of the time it takes humans to learn.

2.2 Practical Deployments

- **Robotics:** In manufacturing or warehouse settings, RL-powered robots can learn to grip irregular objects, navigate crowded floors, and adapt to changing layouts.

- **Healthcare:** RL agents can suggest personalized treatment regimens, "rewarded" for beneficial patient outcomes. Over multiple patients (or simulations), they refine their recommendations.
- **Resource Management:** Energy systems or data centers use RL to balance load and minimize costs. By monitoring energy consumption and performance data, an agent learns how to efficiently allocate resources.
- **Finance:** While algorithmic trading typically relies on a variety of methods, some hedge funds and trading platforms leverage RL to adaptively manage portfolios based on market changes.

3. Multi-Agent Systems: When AI Agents Collaborate (or Compete)

While RL often focuses on single-agent scenarios, many real-world challenges involve multiple agents—consider a team of drones delivering supplies, or autonomous cars negotiating a busy intersection. *Multi-agent systems* explore how multiple intelligent entities can coexist in the same environment, either by cooperating toward a shared goal or competing against each other for limited resources.

3.1 Cooperation vs. Competition

1. **Cooperative Multi-Agent Systems:** Agents share information and work together to optimize a joint reward. Picture a swarm of drones mapping a disaster zone; each drone passes along the data it collects, helping the swarm piece together a global understanding of the area.

2. **Competitive Multi-Agent Systems:** Agents vie for individual rewards. Stock-trading bots might each try to maximize profits at the expense of others, leading to complex market dynamics that reflect real-life competition among traders.
3. **Mixed Settings:** Many scenarios combine both cooperation and competition. For example, in a multi-player video game, agents might form temporary alliances (cooperation) while still competing for overall victory.

3.2 How Multi-Agent RL Works

Multi-agent RL extends the principles of single-agent RL. Each agent observes its local state, chooses actions, and receives rewards. However, the environment's dynamics now include actions by other agents, which can drastically impact the outcome. Strategies evolve as agents learn to predict or adapt to the behavior of others. In some cases, emergent behaviors arise—like spontaneous teamwork or specialization among agents—even when no designer explicitly programmed such outcomes.

3.3 Potential Applications

- **Smart Cities:** Coordinating traffic lights, garbage collection, and emergency services. Agents can share real-time data and reroute resources to address issues, reducing congestion and waste.
- **Logistics:** Fleets of delivery robots or autonomous trucks can coordinate routes to efficiently distribute goods across a region.

- **Search and Rescue:** Multiple robots or drones can split up tasks—some scanning for survivors, others delivering supplies—without overlapping efforts, saving critical time.
- **Game Development and Simulation:** Multi-agent RL helps developers create more realistic and challenging AI opponents or teammates, enhancing player engagement and realism.

4. Emergent Intelligence: Beyond the Sum of the Parts

One of the most intriguing aspects of multi-agent systems is the potential for *emergent intelligence*. In nature, flocking birds or swarming insects display collective behaviors that seem intelligent, despite each individual following simple rules. AI researchers aim to replicate such emergent coordination, hoping that large groups of AI agents can solve problems too complex for any single agent.

4.1 Swarm Intelligence

"Swarm intelligence" refers to the collective behavior of decentralized agents. Each agent follows local rules (e.g., "stay close to neighbors but don't collide") and communicates minimal information, yet the entire group performs complex tasks—like mapping a hazardous environment quickly. Such bottom-up approaches can be robust to failures—if one drone malfunctions, others can continue.

4.2 Unexpected Collaboration or Conflict

Because multi-agent systems can learn and adapt independently, they might develop strategies their programmers never anticipated. In cooperative scenarios, that can be beneficial—a surprising new tactic that outperforms human-designed strategies. But in competitive settings, emergent conflict can lead to high stakes. For instance, if trading bots collectively learn manipulative strategies, the financial system could become more volatile or biased.

5. Challenges in Reinforcement Learning and Multi-Agent Systems

5.1 Scalability and Complexity

As the number of agents or the complexity of the environment grows, so does the computational burden. Training a single RL agent can already require immense processing power, particularly for tasks like image-based control. With multiple agents interacting, the complexity multiplies. Researchers investigate more efficient algorithms and hardware accelerations (like specialized AI chips) to manage these demands.

5.2 Non-Stationarity

In multi-agent RL, the environment is constantly changing because other agents are also learning. This "non-stationary" setting makes it harder for each agent to converge on a stable strategy. Think of a card game: if one player changes tactics midway, everyone else must adapt or risk losing.

5.3 Safety and Reliability

When AI agents have the power to make autonomous decisions in the real world—driving cars, coordinating drones, or managing utility grids—safety is paramount. RL agents learn through trial and error, but errors in the physical world can be costly or even dangerous. Researchers often rely on **simulation** to let agents practice in a safe virtual environment, but bridging the gap from simulation to reality presents its own set of challenges.

5.4 Ethical and Societal Implications

Multi-agent systems can magnify the ethical dilemmas we discussed in earlier chapters. If a swarm of delivery drones clogs the skies, how do we manage air traffic safety or noise pollution? If competing AI systems in finance engage in manipulative trading, who's accountable for the ripple effects on the broader economy? Ensuring these agents operate in alignment with societal values requires a blend of regulatory oversight, technical guardrails, and ongoing public dialogue.

6. Cutting-Edge Research Areas

6.1 Hierarchical Reinforcement Learning

In hierarchical RL, agents break tasks into sub-goals. Instead of learning to "win a complex game" directly, an agent might first learn smaller tasks like "gather resources" or "build a defensive structure." By mastering these subtasks, the agent can tackle the overarching goal more efficiently—much like a person learning a new sport by first practicing basic drills before playing full games.

6.2 Meta-Learning ("Learning to Learn")

Meta-learning agents can adapt quickly to new tasks, often after seeing just a few examples. Rather than mastering a single environment, the agent learns how to learn. Picture a robot that, after being taught how to stack blocks, can swiftly pick up how to sort them by color—even though it never saw colored blocks before. This adaptability is crucial for AI systems expected to operate in unpredictable, real-world conditions.

6.3 Human-Agent Interaction and Shared Autonomy

Another frontier involves blending human expertise with AI adaptivity in real time. For instance, in robotic teleoperation, a human might remotely control a surgical robot with assistance from an AI agent that corrects for jittery hand movements or suggests optimal tool angles. Researchers strive for smooth handoffs between manual control and AI autonomy, aiming to enhance outcomes and reduce cognitive load on human operators.

7. Potential for Transformative Applications

7.1 Global Crisis Response

From pandemics to natural disasters, multi-agent RL systems could coordinate resource distribution, medical triage, and rescue missions on an unprecedented scale. An AI-driven swarm might rapidly map flooded areas, relay critical supplies, and guide people to safe zones—all while adjusting to ongoing threats in real time.

7.2 Autonomous Collaboration in Space

Space agencies like NASA and private companies like SpaceX increasingly rely on autonomous systems for missions beyond Earth. In the future, fleets of AI-driven rovers could coordinate on planetary exploration—sharing data to map unknown terrains, search for signs of life, or build habitat structures for human colonies.

7.3 Climate and Environmental Management

AI agents could help optimize resource use and protect ecosystems. For instance, in agriculture, multi-agent drones might coordinate irrigation schedules, spot pest infestations, and pollinate crops. In wildlife conservation, agents could track endangered species and respond to poaching threats more effectively than lone human rangers can.

8. Looking Ahead: Balancing Promise and Caution

The evolution of reinforcement learning and multi-agent systems underscores AI's enormous potential, but it also highlights the need for thoughtful deployment. As these agents become better at strategic thinking and collaboration, they also become less predictable to their human creators. On one hand, that unpredictability can lead to spectacular breakthroughs—like AlphaGo's imaginative moves that stunned expert Go players. On the other, it can create vulnerabilities and ethical dilemmas, especially if these agents act in ways that humans fail to anticipate or control.

8.1 Governance and Guidelines

Given the complexity and potential risks, robust guidelines for developing and deploying multi-agent RL systems become imperative. Policymakers, industry leaders, and researchers can collaborate on:

- **International Standards:** Setting baseline safety and transparency requirements for multi-agent systems.
- **Shared Simulations and Open Data:** Encouraging open-source tools so that smaller organizations and researchers worldwide can experiment responsibly, rather than allowing only large corporations or governments to drive progress.
- **Risk Assessments:** Employing scenario planning to anticipate how these agents might fail or behave unexpectedly in critical infrastructures like energy grids or healthcare systems.

8.2 Continued Human Oversight

Despite their autonomy, AI agents still need human guidance, especially in high-stakes or ethically sensitive domains. Hybrid models—where humans set overarching goals and values while AI systems handle operational details—can keep development aligned with human interests. By instituting "human-in-the-loop" checkpoints, organizations can maintain a measure of control while still leveraging AI's speed and adaptability.

9. Key Takeaways

1. **Reinforcement Learning (RL):** A technique where agents learn optimal actions by receiving rewards, enabling them to adapt to dynamic environments without relying solely on labeled data.
2. **Multi-Agent Systems:** Multiple agents can collaborate or compete, leading to emergent behaviors that might solve complex, large-scale problems—or create new challenges.
3. **Emergent Intelligence:** When many simple agents work together, they can produce group behaviors that appear more sophisticated than any individual agent's capabilities.
4. **Cutting-Edge Research:** Areas like hierarchical RL, meta-learning, and human-agent collaboration push the boundaries of what AI can achieve in unstructured and dynamic scenarios.
5. **Potential Applications:** From disaster response to resource management, multi-agent RL could drastically improve how we tackle large, complex tasks.
6. **Challenges and Risks:** Scalability, non-stationary environments, ethical dilemmas, and safety are major hurdles requiring technical innovations and responsible governance.

10. Conclusion

Reinforcement learning and multi-agent collaboration propel AI beyond isolated, single-task systems into the realm of adaptive, cooperative, and—at times—unpredictable intelligence. By learning through experience, solving problems with limited human input, and coordinating at scale, these technologies have the capacity to tackle some of the world's most intricate challenges. Yet their power also invites fresh ethical, safety, and governance questions, underscoring the need for prudent design and oversight.

As we continue this journey, the final chapters will explore how these advanced capabilities tie into the broader AI ecosystem—considering infrastructural needs, adoption strategies for businesses, and a future vision of how AI agents might reshape daily life for billions of people. Ultimately, the potential of AI to do good grows in tandem with our responsibility to guide it wisely, ensuring that these revolutionary techniques serve humanity rather than undermine it.

10

Building a Holistic AI Ecosystem

In previous chapters, we've examined the inner workings of AI agents, their applications across industries, their ethical dimensions, and the promise of emerging techniques like reinforcement learning and multi-agent systems. Yet even the most sophisticated AI algorithm is only as effective as the environment in which it operates. Building an **AI ecosystem** goes far beyond installing software or spinning up a few servers in the cloud. It involves carefully orchestrating data pipelines, computing infrastructure, interoperability standards, and collaborative networks that help AI flourish at scale. This chapter explains how businesses, researchers, governments, and citizens can cultivate an environment where AI agents can be developed responsibly and used effectively—ultimately reaping the transformative benefits these technologies can offer.

1. Why a Holistic Ecosystem Matters

Just as a plant won't thrive without the right soil, sunlight, and water, AI agents can't reach their full potential in isolation. An ecosystem approach acknowledges that AI success depends on multiple interdependent elements:

1. **Computing Power and Infrastructure:** From GPUs and specialized chips to distributed cloud environments, AI workloads can be demanding, and the right infrastructure is essential for training and running large models.
2. **Data Pipelines and Quality:** High-quality, well-governed data serves as the fuel for AI, whether for supervised learning, reinforcement learning, or real-time inference.
3. **Interoperability and Standards:** AI agents often need to communicate with other systems—sometimes from different vendors or across national borders. Common standards enable seamless data exchange and collaboration.
4. **Human and Organizational Factors:** The best technology can falter if organizations lack the expertise, culture, or governance to implement it ethically and effectively.
5. **Regulatory and Ethical Frameworks:** Guidelines and enforcement ensure that AI-driven innovations protect privacy, reduce bias, and maintain public trust.

When these elements align, AI can move from siloed prototypes to integrated, transformative solutions that reshape entire industries and address complex global challenges.

2. Infrastructure Requirements: Cloud, Edge, and Beyond

2.1 The Rise of Cloud Computing

A central piece of the AI ecosystem puzzle is the *cloud*. Platforms like Amazon Web Services (AWS), Microsoft Azure, and Google Cloud allow businesses to lease massive amounts of computing power on demand. This flexibility is crucial for AI training, which can be computationally intensive. Deep learning models, especially those dealing with image recognition or natural language processing, often require powerful hardware accelerators such as GPUs or TPUs (Tensor Processing Units).

Why Cloud Matters for AI

1. **Scalability:** Companies can instantly spin up or shut down hundreds of GPU-accelerated servers for training tasks, paying only for what they use.
2. **Collaboration:** Developers from different parts of the world can work on the same cloud-based platform, sharing datasets and model checkpoints easily.
3. **Lower Entry Barriers:** Startups and small research teams no longer need to purchase expensive hardware upfront to experiment with AI.

2.2 Edge Computing for Real-Time Insights

While the cloud excels at large-scale processing, some AI tasks demand *immediate* responses, minimal latency, or offline capabilities. **Edge computing** pushes computation closer to where data is generated—on devices like smartphones, IoT sensors, or autonomous machines. This approach reduces the need to send all data back to a distant data center.

Typical Edge Scenarios

- **Autonomous Vehicles:** Self-driving cars must make split-second decisions even in areas with poor connectivity. Processing sensor data locally is often more reliable than waiting for cloud instructions.
- **Industrial IoT:** In manufacturing or energy sectors, devices on the factory floor can analyze operational data in real time, predicting machine failures without a constant high-bandwidth connection to a cloud server.
- **Smartphones and Wearables:** Apps that provide on-device AI features—like voice assistants or health monitoring—offer immediate feedback and improved privacy by limiting data transmission to the cloud.

2.3 Hybrid Approaches

In many cases, organizations adopt a **hybrid** strategy, using both cloud and edge computing. Data might be processed locally for speed and privacy, then aggregated and analyzed in the cloud for deeper insights. For example, a fleet of drones could process immediate sensor data at the edge for navigation, while uploading key metrics to the cloud for global coordination or long-term trend analysis.

3. Data Pipelines: From Collection to Governance

3.1 Building Reliable Pipelines

For an AI agent to learn effectively, it needs consistent, high-quality data. However, data often arrives from disparate sources—a CRM system here, a sensor network there—sometimes in inconsistent formats. Constructing robust **data pipelines** involves:

1. **Extraction:** Pulling data from various sources (databases, APIs, streaming platforms).
2. **Transformation:** Cleaning, normalizing, and combining data. This may include resolving missing values, converting formats, or deduplicating records.
3. **Loading and Storage:** Sending the refined data to a centralized location—often a data lake or warehouse—where AI models can access it.

Data pipelines must be reliable, scalable, and secure, ensuring minimal downtime and protecting sensitive information. Tools like Apache Kafka (for streaming data), Spark (for big data processing), or Airflow (for workflow management) have become the backbone of AI-driven operations.

3.2 Data Governance and Ethical Handling

Collecting massive amounts of personal or proprietary data raises privacy and ethical concerns. Regulations like the EU's General Data Protection Regulation (GDPR) mandate strict guidelines for how organizations handle personal information, requiring transparency and consent. Businesses that ignore privacy rules can face hefty fines and reputational damage.

Key Steps in Ethical Data Management

- **Consent and Transparency:** Clearly inform users about what data is collected and how it's used.
- **Anonymization:** Strip out identifiable information when using datasets for AI training to protect user privacy.
- **Access Control:** Limit who can view or modify data, ensuring only authorized personnel or systems have access.
- **Retention Policies:** Delete data that's no longer necessary to minimize risks of misuse or breaches.

Strong data governance not only mitigates risks but also builds trust, facilitating smoother adoption of AI solutions in sensitive areas like healthcare or finance.

4. Interoperability: Speaking the Same Language

4.1 Standard Protocols and Frameworks

AI agents often need to interact with various services: databases, sensors, user interfaces, or even other AI systems. Ensuring these components communicate seamlessly requires **interoperability** standards. Imagine a multinational logistics company using AI to optimize shipping routes: the central AI engine must gather real-time data from trucks, cargo ships, and warehouses across continents, each possibly running different software.

Common Interoperability Tools

- **APIs (Application Programming Interfaces):** Well-documented APIs let AI agents request data or services from different platforms in a consistent way.

- **Messaging Protocols (e.g., MQTT, AMQP):** Ideal for IoT devices, these protocols enable lightweight, real-time communication with minimal overhead.
- **Data Formats (JSON, XML, Protocol Buffers):** Agreeing on a standard data format reduces confusion and conversion errors.

4.2 Open Standards and Collaboration

Industry consortia and standards bodies like ISO, IEEE, or W3C are increasingly focusing on AI-related guidelines—covering everything from model representation to ethical compliance. Open standards help smaller players integrate with larger ecosystems, leveling the playing field. They also reduce vendor lock-in, encouraging healthy competition and faster innovation.

5. The Role of Open Source

5.1 Accelerating Innovation

Open-source software—where the source code is freely available—plays a pivotal part in AI development. Frameworks like TensorFlow, PyTorch, and scikit-learn let developers build, train, and deploy models without reinventing the wheel. These tools empower researchers, startups, and hobbyists to experiment with state-of-the-art algorithms, often with just a laptop and an internet connection.

Open source fosters a **virtuous cycle** of collaboration: improvements made by one team can be shared and built upon by others, accelerating the overall pace of innovation. This community-driven approach spreads knowledge quickly and breaks down barriers to entry.

5.2 Community and Knowledge Sharing

Open-source communities aren't just about code; they're about **people**—data scientists, software engineers, domain experts—exchanging ideas. Conferences, forums, and hackathons become breeding grounds for new techniques and best practices. For instance, GitHub, Kaggle, and Stack Overflow host countless projects and discussions on everything from deep learning architectures to niche reinforcement learning problems. Such collaboration helps standardize best practices and fosters a culture of openness that can steer AI in more socially beneficial directions.

6. Fostering Partnerships: Academia, Industry, and Government

6.1 Academia's Crucial Role

Universities and research institutes have historically driven foundational AI breakthroughs, from early neural network concepts to modern reinforcement learning achievements. Academic labs often focus on long-term, high-risk research that might not yield immediate commercial returns—think of the early stages of deep learning when it wasn't yet profitable. By partnering with academia, companies gain access to emerging ideas and talent, while universities benefit from real-world data and funding. This synergy can propel AI research forward in leaps rather than incremental steps.

6.2 Corporate Collaborations

It's becoming increasingly common for corporations to join forces on AI initiatives, even if they're competitors in other areas. For example, rivals in the automotive sector might collaborate on self-driving vehicle standards to ensure safety and interoperability on public roads. Similarly, cross-industry coalitions can share anonymized datasets to tackle major challenges like climate change or pandemics. By pooling resources, these partnerships can undertake ambitious projects that would be too costly or risky for a single organization.

6.3 Government and Public Sector Support

Governments play a pivotal role in shaping the AI ecosystem. Alongside setting regulations, they can fund research grants, provide tax incentives for AI startups, or build data infrastructure accessible to the public. Some nations even establish specialized AI hubs or "innovation zones" to attract global talent. When done thoughtfully, government support can ensure that AI development aligns with societal goals—expanding access, creating jobs, and addressing national or regional challenges (e.g., improving healthcare or transforming agriculture).

7. Cultivating the Human Dimension

7.1 Organizational Culture and Training

Even the most advanced AI tools can falter if an organization lacks **digital literacy** and a culture that embraces technological change. Employees may resist adopting AI out of fear for their jobs or misunderstanding of how these systems operate. Clear communication, hands-on training, and a culture that values experimentation and learning can bridge these gaps.

Leaders who prioritize **cross-functional collaboration**—bringing together data scientists, subject-matter experts, and frontline workers—are more likely to spot AI opportunities that deliver real value. By involving employees in the design process, organizations increase buy-in and can better align AI implementations with practical needs.

7.2 Ethics, Accountability, and Inclusivity

A holistic ecosystem respects not only technical best practices but also human values. Ensuring that AI agents do not discriminate, infringe on privacy, or undermine user autonomy requires continuous vigilance. Building *responsible AI* might include:

- **Ethical Review Boards:** Internal committees that assess potential societal impacts before launching a new AI tool.
- **Transparency Reports:** Publicly disclosing how AI systems make decisions, particularly in sensitive areas like healthcare, finance, or policing.
- **Inclusion Initiatives:** Recruiting diverse teams to reduce the risk of biased data sets and algorithms.

Organizations that integrate ethics from the ground up—rather than tacking it on at the end—are more likely to earn public trust and avoid backlash.

8. Roadblocks and Future Directions

8.1 Overcoming Fragmentation

As AI technologies evolve, the ecosystem can become fragmented—multiple platforms, vendor-specific standards, and competing frameworks. This patchwork can impede seamless integration and raise costs. Calls for **open interoperability** are growing, but progress requires consensus across stakeholders. Ongoing dialogue among standards bodies, researchers, and industry groups can help unify best practices.

8.2 Balancing Efficiency with Sustainability

AI training can be energy-intensive, sometimes leaving a notable environmental footprint. Building a responsible ecosystem means investing in *greener* data centers, optimizing algorithms for efficiency, and exploring low-power hardware. Innovations like specialized chips for matrix operations (e.g., Google's TPU) already reduce energy consumption compared to general-purpose CPUs, but more can be done to measure and mitigate AI's carbon costs.

8.3 Evolving Governance Models

Regulating AI is a moving target. Rapid advances in deep learning, natural language processing, and multi-agent systems challenge existing frameworks. Policymakers often struggle to keep pace, making laws that either stifle innovation or leave dangerous gaps. Future governance models might involve **dynamic regulations** that update as AI capabilities change—coupled with robust oversight mechanisms, from algorithmic audits to citizen review panels.

9. Key Takeaways

1. **Infrastructure Is Paramount:** Cloud computing, edge devices, and hybrid approaches form the backbone for AI training and deployment.
2. **Data Pipelines and Governance:** Reliable data streams and ethical data handling practices are essential for high-quality AI outputs.
3. **Interoperability:** Standard protocols, open APIs, and shared data formats enable AI agents and services to communicate fluidly, spurring ecosystem growth.
4. **Open Source and Collaboration:** Community-driven innovation accelerates AI progress, while partnerships among academia, industry, and government expand both resources and ambition.
5. **Human-Centric Focus:** AI ecosystems thrive best when organizations foster digital literacy, embed ethics from the start, and ensure diverse stakeholder engagement.
6. **Future Challenges:** As AI advances, so must governance, sustainability efforts, and consensus on standards to prevent fragmentation and maintain public trust.

10. Conclusion

Building a holistic AI ecosystem is about more than just technology. It's about weaving together the threads of infrastructure, data quality, collaboration, interoperability, and ethical culture. When these elements align, AI can move from isolated pilot projects to an omnipresent force—one that helps solve pressing problems in healthcare, education, transportation, and beyond.

The best AI strategies won't emerge from any single player or siloed approach. Success requires a network of contributors—research labs, startups, industry titans, nonprofits, and government agencies—working in concert. And as advanced as AI systems become, the human factor remains pivotal: *people* must steer these technologies responsibly, ensuring that they serve broad societal interests rather than merely amplifying existing power structures.

In our next chapter, we'll explore practical adoption strategies for businesses and organizations aiming to integrate AI into their operations. From identifying the right use cases to managing pilot projects and scaling effectively, we'll provide a roadmap for transitioning from AI curiosity to AI-driven transformation. By grasping both the technical and organizational dimensions of AI deployment, you can position yourself—and your enterprise—to thrive in a world where intelligent agents are rapidly becoming essential partners in progress.

11

Paths to Adoption: Strategies for Businesses and Organizations

Bringing AI agents into an organization isn't a matter of simply flipping a switch and letting intelligent algorithms do their work. It requires a calculated approach that aligns technical capabilities with strategic goals, operational realities, and a culture willing to embrace change. While the transformative potential of AI is vast, so are the pitfalls of poor planning—from failed pilot programs to ethical missteps. In this chapter, we'll examine practical strategies for businesses and other organizations that seek to integrate AI successfully. We'll explore how to identify the right use cases, build an implementation roadmap, manage common challenges, and continuously refine AI deployments for maximum impact.

1. Identifying High-Value Use Cases

1.1 Aligning AI with Organizational Goals

A major risk for AI adoption is jumping into the latest trend without a clear sense of *why* or *how* it supports broader objectives. Before selecting a use case, leadership should articulate how AI aligns with the organization's strategic priorities. Are you aiming to reduce operational costs, improve customer experiences, drive innovation, or open new revenue streams? Answering these questions helps narrow the focus to areas where AI can offer tangible, measurable outcomes.

Examples of Strategic AI Goals

- **Cost Reduction:** Automating invoice processing or supply chain logistics.
- **Customer Experience:** Deploying chatbots or recommendation systems to improve service.
- **Operational Efficiency:** Using predictive maintenance on manufacturing lines or energy grids.
- **Innovation:** Exploring new products, like personalized healthcare plans or smart-home solutions.

1.2 Evaluating Feasibility and ROI

Once you have a shortlist of potential AI projects, evaluate them on two dimensions: **feasibility** and **impact**. Feasibility factors might include the availability of data, existing infrastructure, and in-house expertise. Impact typically revolves around the potential return on investment (ROI), whether in cost savings, revenue gains, or strategic differentiation. A simple scoring model—where each proposed project is rated on these dimensions—can help teams decide which AI initiatives are most likely to deliver real value.

Practical Questions

- **Data Readiness:** Do we have clean, relevant, and sufficiently large datasets?
- **Talent and Tools:** Does our workforce possess the AI and data-engineering skills required? If not, can we train them or hire externally?
- **Timeline and Risk:** How quickly must the project show results? Are there regulatory or technical risks to consider?

2. Implementation Roadmap: From Concept to Full Deployment

2.1 The Pilot Phase

Starting small with a **pilot program** is usually the safest route. This proof-of-concept allows teams to test AI models on a limited scale, validate assumptions, and gauge the feasibility of a full deployment.

1. **Define Success Criteria:** Choose clear metrics—like accuracy rates, cost savings, or user satisfaction—that determine if the pilot meets expectations.
2. **Assemble a Cross-Functional Team:** AI projects benefit from diverse perspectives, including data engineers, domain experts, and end users. Close collaboration ensures the pilot addresses real-world needs.
3. **Iterate Rapidly:** Use agile methods, running short development sprints to refine the model. Early user feedback can reveal hidden pitfalls or highlight unanticipated benefits.

2.2 Scaling Up

If the pilot demonstrates promise, the next step is to **scale up**. This often involves integrating the AI solution into core workflows or consumer-facing platforms. Key considerations include:

- **Infrastructure:** Ensure servers, cloud resources, or on-premise hardware can handle increased traffic.
- **Data Pipeline Upgrades:** Moving from a pilot dataset to live production data demands robust ingestion, cleaning, and governance processes.
- **User Training:** Employees interacting with AI (e.g., a call center agent assisted by a recommendation engine) need guidance on how to use the new system effectively.
- **Change Management:** Successful rollouts often require rethinking job roles, incentivizing adoption, and mitigating fear of automation.

2.3 Continuous Monitoring and Improvement

AI agents aren't "set-and-forget" technologies. Over time, data distributions can shift—imagine a recommendation system that needs to adapt to changing consumer trends. Regular performance checks help maintain accuracy and reliability.

Continuous Improvement Tactics

- **Performance Dashboards:** Real-time metrics for decision-makers to catch early signs of drifting accuracy or rising error rates.
- **Version Control and Model Retraining:** Periodically update

models with fresh data or new techniques, archiving old versions for reference.

- **User Feedback Loops:** Involve frontline staff or customers in reporting anomalies or suggestions. This direct input often catches issues that purely technical monitoring overlooks.

3. Challenges and Best Practices

3.1 Common Pitfalls

1. **Data Issues:** Many AI projects fail due to insufficient or poor-quality data. Even if data exists, it may be siloed, inconsistent, or non-representative.
2. **Overly Ambitious Projects:** Organizations sometimes try to launch AI in a mission-critical domain without the necessary groundwork. A high-profile failure can set back AI adoption by years.
3. **Lack of Stakeholder Buy-In:** Top-down mandates that ignore end-user needs risk low adoption. AI must address real pain points to gain acceptance.
4. **Ethical Oversight Gaps:** AI systems that inadvertently violate privacy or embed bias can damage reputations and invite regulatory scrutiny.

3.2 Strategies for Success

- **Start Small, Scale Fast:** Begin with pilots that are ambitious enough to be meaningful but narrow enough to be manageable.
- **Data Governance:** Invest early in data cleaning, integra-

tion, and stewardship. Cloud-based data lakes or well-maintained data warehouses can streamline future AI efforts.

- **Transparency and Communication:** Keep employees informed about how AI is being used, what it can (and cannot) do, and how it might change their roles.
- **Ethical Guardrails:** Appoint ethics committees or designate "AI ambassadors" who ensure projects respect privacy, fairness, and accountability.
- **Cross-Functional Collaboration:** Technical teams and domain experts should co-own AI initiatives. The best insights often come from the intersection of deep technology and business or field expertise.

4. Case Studies and Lessons Learned

4.1 Retail: Personalization Engine Success

A mid-size online retailer sought to improve customer engagement and sales by deploying an AI-driven recommendation engine. Here's how they approached it:

1. **Pilot:** They ran a three-month pilot suggesting personalized product picks for a subset of returning customers.
2. **Data Preparation:** A cross-functional team spent weeks cleaning up purchase histories and clickstream logs to remove duplicates and irrelevant entries.
3. **Results:** During the pilot, conversion rates rose by 15%. Customers spent more time on the site, exploring suggested items.
4. **Scale-Up:** Encouraged by the pilot, the retailer fully

integrated the recommendation system into its homepage and email campaigns. They also added real-time AI that adapts suggestions based on current browsing behavior.

5. **Key Takeaway:** Transparent communication with customers about the recommendation system increased trust. Opt-out options and data privacy assurances helped avoid pushback.

4.2 Manufacturing: Predictive Maintenance

A large automotive parts manufacturer introduced an AI solution for predictive maintenance:

1. **Use Case Identification:** High costs were linked to unexpected machine downtime. An AI approach offered a way to predict failures before they occurred.
2. **Pilot:** A single production line was equipped with IoT sensors, sending temperature and vibration data to a cloud-based AI model.
3. **Outcome:** The pilot flagged anomalies that, if unaddressed, would have led to a major malfunction within days. Maintenance teams intervened early, saving thousands of dollars in repair costs.
4. **Scale-Up:** The manufacturer rolled out similar sensor setups across other lines and plants, tailoring the model to each environment's unique patterns.
5. **Key Takeaway:** Collaboration between engineers, data scientists, and frontline mechanics was crucial. Mechanics provided domain-specific insights that refined the model's accuracy.

5. Overcoming Organizational Resistance

5.1 Fear of Job Loss and Cultural Barriers

Workers sometimes view AI as a threat, fearing layoffs or a devaluation of their skills. Addressing these concerns head-on can make or break an AI project. Leaders should clarify that AI typically *augments* human roles, automating repetitive tasks and freeing employees to focus on complex, creative, or customer-facing work. If job shifts are inevitable, proactive reskilling and outplacement support foster goodwill and maintain morale.

Addressing Resistance

- **Transparent Communication:** Share details about how AI will impact roles, timelines, and the broader strategic picture.
- **Pilot Success Stories:** Highlight employees who have thrived using AI tools, reinforcing the narrative of augmentation.
- **Upskilling Programs:** Offer training or career development pathways that help workers acquire AI-related competencies.

5.2 Building a Learning Culture

AI thrives in environments that value experimentation, continuous learning, and cross-functional collaboration. Some organizations establish internal "AI guilds" or learning communities, where interested staff can attend workshops, collaborate on hackathons, and share project updates. This grassroots engagement helps spread AI awareness beyond a small data science team, embedding innovation deeper into the organizational fabric.

6. Scaling AI Responsibly

6.1 Ensuring Fairness and Inclusivity

As AI becomes more intertwined with decision-making—such as hiring, lending, or healthcare—organizations have a moral and legal obligation to prevent biased outcomes. This can be especially critical when scaling solutions beyond initial pilots.

- **Bias Audits:** Regularly analyze the model's predictions across different demographic segments.
- **Diverse Teams:** Involving people from varied backgrounds in AI design can catch potential biases early.
- **Regulatory Compliance:** Keep abreast of laws on data protection, equal opportunity, and consumer protection to avoid legal pitfalls.

6.2 Environmental Footprint

Training large AI models can consume substantial energy, especially if run frequently or on massive datasets. As organizations scale their AI usage, energy costs and carbon footprints grow too. Strategies like **model compression**, **efficient data sampling**, and **using renewable energy sources** for data centers can help reduce the environmental impact, aligning AI adoption with sustainability goals.

6.3 Ethical Reviews and Long-Term Impacts

Some organizations create **ethics committees** or "Responsible AI offices" to review major AI deployments. These bodies weigh potential long-term impacts on society, the environment, and various stakeholders. While critics might see these measures as slowing innovation, careful review can prevent reputational damage and align AI-driven projects with core organizational values.

7. Continuous Improvement and Future-Proofing

7.1 Monitoring Evolving Technologies

AI doesn't stand still. Breakthroughs in reinforcement learning, multi-agent coordination, or large-scale language models can quickly render existing solutions outdated. Organizations that consistently track advancements can capitalize on new techniques—like improved training methods or hardware accelerators—to refine and modernize their AI deployments. This requires dedicated resources for research, experimentation, and **proof-of-concept** trials.

7.2 Feedback Loops with Users

When AI tools interact directly with customers—like chatbots or recommendation engines—regular user feedback is invaluable. Analytics on user satisfaction, dropout rates, or service complaints can reveal whether the system is truly meeting needs. Even internal-facing AI systems, such as HR analytics or finance automation, benefit from structured feedback processes. Keeping a user-centric lens ensures that AI evolves in line with genuine needs rather than drifting into "automation for automation's sake."

7.3 Collaborative Roadmaps

A long-term AI roadmap helps ensure that each new project or pilot aligns with an overarching vision. This roadmap should be flexible enough to accommodate emerging technologies and lessons learned from prior rollouts. By working collaboratively with stakeholders—from the C-suite and legal teams to front-line managers and data scientists—organizations can maintain a living, breathing plan that evolves with real-world conditions.

8. Key Takeaways

1. **Value-Driven Use Cases:** AI initiatives should stem from clear business or organizational objectives, validated by feasibility and ROI considerations.
2. **Pilot, Scale, Refine:** Starting small allows quick learning and lowers risk, while a successful pilot paves the way for broader deployment.
3. **Common Pitfalls:** Data quality issues, stakeholder resistance, and ethical oversights can derail AI projects.
4. **Best Practices for Success:** Invest in data governance, cultivate transparency, involve cross-functional teams, and embed ethics from the outset.
5. **Managing Resistance:** Open communication, upskilling, and proof of augmentation (rather than replacement) help ease worker fears.
6. **Responsible Growth:** As AI scales, maintain vigilance on

fairness, sustainability, and user feedback to ensure the technology continues to serve people effectively.

7. **Future-Proofing:** Keep pace with evolving AI research and market trends, adjusting roadmaps and retraining models as new opportunities or challenges arise.

9. Conclusion

The journey to AI adoption is seldom linear. Even with a clear business case and a robust technical strategy, unexpected hurdles—like data bottlenecks or cultural pushback—can emerge. Yet these challenges are surmountable when organizations approach AI with a learning mindset, incrementally building on successes, and proactively addressing concerns around ethics and equity.

By starting with pilots, scaling responsibly, and investing in people's skills, businesses and institutions can maximize AI's transformative potential. They can free up human ingenuity for higher-level tasks, deliver better experiences for customers, reduce operational costs, and spark innovations that might reshape entire industries. Above all, successful AI integration relies on the interplay of technology, culture, governance, and continuous improvement. In our final chapter, we'll look ahead to a future where AI agents shape everyday life even more profoundly—exploring how our societies might evolve as these systems continue to advance and integrate into everything from personal healthcare to large-scale climate modeling.

12

A Glimpse of Tomorrow: How AI Agents Will Reshape Our World

Artificial Intelligence has come a long way from its roots in academic research labs to its current status as a ubiquitous presence in daily life. Smart assistants respond to our voice commands, factories hum with AI-powered robots, and self-driving cars inch ever closer to mainstream adoption. Yet these advances might only be the tip of the iceberg. As AI agents grow more capable, collaborative, and deeply embedded in society, they have the potential to transform nearly every aspect of how we work, learn, travel, and communicate. In this final chapter, we take a future-focused look at how AI agents could reshape our world in the years to come. We'll explore emerging technologies, offer realistic scenarios of how they might evolve, and consider the responsibility we share in guiding AI's unfolding story.

1. The Rise of Truly Smart Cities

Cities are magnets for both people and innovation. Yet they also face immense challenges: traffic congestion, pollution, housing shortages, and strained public services. AI agents can help address these issues by making cities "smarter." Imagine a future metropolis where:

- **Traffic Flow:** AI-driven systems dynamically control traffic lights and autonomous vehicles to minimize congestion, reducing commutes and air pollution.
- **Energy Efficiency:** Sensors in buildings constantly communicate with power grids, letting AI agents balance supply and demand in real time. Lights, heating, and cooling systems adjust automatically based on occupancy.
- **Public Safety:** AI-assisted drones could help locate missing persons or track evolving natural disasters. Law enforcement agencies might use predictive analytics (under ethical and transparent guidelines) to anticipate areas that need heightened attention.

Although some elements of this smart city vision already exist in pilot programs—such as real-time traffic management—widespread adoption faces hurdles. Infrastructure modernization is costly, and privacy concerns loom large. Achieving these visions also requires robust data sharing and cooperation across government agencies, private sectors, and local communities. As AI grows more adept at orchestrating large systems, we could see entire regions become interconnected networks of intelligent services—if we can balance innovation with the public interest.

2. Personalizing Education at Scale

For centuries, education has followed a largely one-size-fits-all model: classrooms with set curricula, group instruction, and standardized testing. But as AI agents become more sophisticated, they could usher in a new era of personalized learning:

- **Adaptive Learning Platforms:** Intelligent tutoring agents can gauge a student's progress, adapting problem sets and pacing to match individual needs. For instance, if a learner struggles with algebraic fractions, the platform can offer extra practice and real-time explanations.
- **Global Access:** In regions with limited access to quality education, AI-driven apps on affordable devices could deliver interactive lessons, bridging gaps in teacher availability.
- **Lifelong Learning:** Workers facing rapid technological changes can benefit from AI-personalized training, seamlessly updating their skills rather than relying solely on formal degrees.

These developments promise a more inclusive and flexible system. However, skepticism remains about how well AI can replace—or even replicate—the nuanced role of human educators. Emotional support, mentorship, and spontaneous classroom discussions might still demand the distinctly human touch. Yet the synergy between teachers and AI agents could lead to hybrid models where AI handles routine assessments and customized lesson planning, freeing educators to concentrate on higher-level mentoring. Over time, this synergy could democratize quality education worldwide—if we ensure equitable access and guard against data exploitation or algorithmic biases.

3. A Revolution in Healthcare and Wellness

Healthcare stands to be one of the most profoundly affected arenas for AI agents. Several transformative trends are already taking shape:

1. **Telehealth and Remote Diagnostics:** AI-powered apps can analyze patient symptoms and vital signs, connecting people with medical professionals from home. Over the next decade, we may see advanced diagnostic agents that scan patient data (like wearable sensor readings or imaging scans) and offer preliminary insights before the patient even schedules a visit.
2. **Precision Medicine:** By sifting through genomic information, AI agents might identify the best treatment plans for each patient's unique genetic profile. Instead of a trial-and-error approach, treatment would be more targeted and personalized.
3. **Proactive Health Management:** Wellness agents could monitor our daily habits—activity level, diet, sleep—and provide nudges to help prevent chronic illnesses. Imagine an AI "coach" that encourages you to take a short walk when your step count is low or suggests healthier meal ideas when your diet needs a boost.

While these advancements promise lower costs and better outcomes, key challenges remain. Privacy is paramount: medical data is among the most sensitive information people hold.

Robust safeguards must be in place to ensure data isn't misused or sold without consent. Additionally, healthcare systems must avoid an overreliance on AI that could devalue human judgment or compassion, especially in cases where emotional support is as important as clinical treatment. Still, if balanced carefully, the integration of AI in healthcare could lead to a new era of wellness focused on prevention, personalization, and patient empowerment.

4. Creative Collaboration with Machines

Until recently, creativity was widely considered a strictly human domain. Yet AI is increasingly producing compelling art, music, and even literature. While many creative AI systems rely on statistical patterns, they're already demonstrating the capacity to surprise and inspire:

- **AI-Generated Art:** Neural network models can mimic artists' styles or create entirely new aesthetic expressions. Some pieces have even sold for high prices at auction, igniting debates about authorship and originality.
- **Music Composition:** AI composers can generate melodies, harmonies, or entire tracks, providing a wellspring of ideas for musicians. Producers might collaborate with these agents to blend their personal flair with algorithmic novelty.
- **Literary Assistance:** Language models can draft story outlines, propose edits, or co-write chapters, much like a human collaborator offering suggestions.

As AI creativity matures, we'll need to redefine what artistic collaboration means. Artists might become curators or directors, guiding AI systems to refine raw outputs and add personal touches. Intellectual property frameworks could also evolve to clarify ownership of works generated partly or wholly by AI. Far from rendering artists obsolete, these tools might empower more people to explore creativity, shaping an era where human–machine co-creation becomes the norm rather than an oddity.

5. Addressing Global Challenges: AI for the Planet

Our planet faces pressing challenges: climate change, resource scarcity, and environmental degradation. AI agents can help tackle these problems by analyzing vast data sets and orchestrating solutions at a scale no single human institution could manage alone:

- **Climate Modeling:** AI can refine predictions about weather patterns, sea-level rise, and carbon emissions, helping policymakers create more targeted interventions.
- **Resource Allocation:** In agriculture, AI-enabled drones and sensors can optimize water usage, reduce pesticide application, and boost crop yields. In fisheries, AI can monitor populations to prevent overfishing and protect marine biodiversity.
- **Disaster Response:** Multi-agent systems can coordinate relief efforts after hurricanes, earthquakes, or pandemics—deploying resources more efficiently to the hardest-hit areas.

While no single technology will solve such colossal challenges on its own, AI can at least provide better tools for informed decision-making. The crux, however, is cooperation. If data remains siloed or if competing interests resist pooling resources, AI's effectiveness diminishes. Genuine global cooperation—through shared data, open platforms, and transnational governance—may be essential for tapping AI's full potential in safeguarding our planet.

6. Potential Pitfalls and Emerging Risks

Even as we celebrate AI's promise, new challenges and risks emerge that require careful navigation:

1. **Algorithmic Manipulation:** As AI systems become integral to finance, media, and politics, bad actors could exploit them for disinformation, market manipulation, or cyber-attacks.
2. **Dependence and Vulnerabilities:** Overreliance on AI systems might lead to complacency or skill erosion among humans. If these systems fail or become compromised, entire infrastructures could be at risk.
3. **Societal Fragmentation:** AI-driven content filtering can create "echo chambers," where people only see viewpoints that reinforce their existing beliefs. This may intensify polarization, undermining social cohesion.
4. **Unintended Consequences:** Complex AI agents, especially in multi-agent systems, can behave in ways that even their developers can't fully predict, raising concerns about unforeseen negative outcomes.

Addressing these threats demands a multi-pronged approach.

Technical measures (like adversarial resilience and rigorous testing) must pair with robust governance frameworks, stakeholder engagement, and continuous public oversight. The future of AI will likely be shaped as much by how we handle these risks as by any specific technological breakthroughs.

7. Societal Shifts and Changing Norms

The proliferation of AI agents may reshape cultural norms, particularly around work and social interactions:

- **Redefining Work:** As mundane tasks become automated, societies may need to value creativity, empathy, and interpersonal skills more than ever. We could see a shift toward "human-centric" roles—counseling, teaching, coaching—that leverage skills machines can't easily replicate.
- **Rethinking Leisure and Purpose:** If AI-driven automation dramatically shortens the workweek, people could have more time for family, hobbies, and community. But how societies structure their economies and social safety nets will determine whether that extra time is widely enjoyed or overshadowed by insecurity.
- **Privacy and Identity:** We increasingly leave digital footprints, from our online interactions to biometric data. AI can piece these fragments into intimate profiles. Societies may debate new norms around anonymity, data ownership, and the right to be forgotten, influencing how we define personal identity in a hyperconnected world.

No single outcome is predestined. While technology shapes possibilities, culture, policy, and individual choice will mediate

AI's ultimate impact on our daily lives. Achieving balanced, inclusive progress requires ongoing dialogue among governments, corporations, researchers, and the public.

8. The Future Workforce: Upskilling and Collaboration

The next wave of AI could reshape occupations in ways we can't fully anticipate. Yet certain trends are already apparent:

1. **Data Literacy Becomes Ubiquitous:** In a world teeming with AI-driven insights, even non-technical roles may require comfort with data interpretation. Schools and professional training programs must adapt accordingly.
2. **Cross-Disciplinary Roles:** AI might fuse with engineering, healthcare, finance, and the arts, spawning hybrid careers like "AI ethicist," "machine learning translator," or "healthcare data strategist."
3. **Human–Machine Pairing:** In fields like manufacturing or customer service, a single human employee might oversee multiple AI agents—managing exceptions and adding empathic or creative elements where algorithms fall short.

This evolving workforce could bring major benefits—higher productivity, better customer experiences, fresh career pathways—provided we mitigate displacement effects for those whose jobs are lost or fundamentally altered. Lifelong learning, supported by governments and industries, may become the norm as each wave of AI demands new competencies.

9. Balancing Power and Caution

AI's rapid evolution is reminiscent of past industrial revolutions that dramatically reshaped societies. Yet the speed and scale of AI's potential impact may dwarf earlier transformations. The flipside of rapid innovation is the risk of catastrophic misuse if guidelines and safeguards lag behind. Key considerations include:

- **Ethical and Inclusive Design:** Developers should embed fairness, transparency, and inclusivity from the start, rather than treating them as afterthoughts.
- **Regulatory Foresight:** Policymakers need agility to adapt laws and frameworks as AI progresses, ensuring they don't stifle beneficial innovations while still protecting people and society.
- **Public Engagement:** Citizens should remain informed and engaged, pressing for accountability, privacy, and equitable access to AI benefits. Grassroots movements and civic tech initiatives can help democratize AI.

If society can strike the right balance between harnessing AI's power and applying well-considered caution, we stand to gain a future where AI genuinely enhances human well-being rather than undermining it.

10. Scenarios for 2030 and Beyond

It's easy to make bold predictions about the future, but equally easy to be wrong. Nonetheless, scenario thinking helps us visualize possibilities:

1. **Optimistic Harmony:** AI-driven solutions dramatically lower carbon emissions, manage disease outbreaks, and create new industries. Wealth grows more evenly, thanks to robust social policies and global collaboration. Human creativity, freed from repetitive tasks, flourishes.
2. **Bifurcated World:** AI becomes accessible mostly to tech-savvy or wealthy populations. Economic inequalities worsen, fueling social unrest. Nations lacking AI infrastructure or expertise face marginalization.
3. **Surveillance States:** Governments or corporate giants leverage AI for extensive monitoring, controlling dissent or shaping public opinion. Privacy erodes, trust in institutions plummets, and democracy weakens.
4. **Resilient Adaptation:** Through incremental, carefully regulated progress, societies adapt to AI's disruptions. Job markets transform but produce enough pathways for reskilling. AI is widely used but remains under human oversight, preserving social cohesion.

Which scenario emerges depends not just on technology but on the social, economic, and political choices we make over the next decade. By staying engaged in these decisions, we can steer AI's trajectory closer to the more inclusive, empowering futures and away from dystopian pitfalls.

11. A Collective Responsibility

As we reflect on AI's trajectory, one theme recurs: *no single entity controls AI's fate.* Researchers, entrepreneurs, policymakers, educators, consumers—all shape how AI evolves and is used. While engineers and data scientists build algorithms, politicians decide on regulation and funding, and the public voices support or concern through market behavior and civic activism. The interplay of these forces determines AI's real-world outcomes.

To ensure AI remains a force for good, we must cultivate a culture of **responsible innovation**:

- **Open Dialogues:** Engage communities, not just experts, in discussions about AI's benefits and risks.
- **Transparent Practices:** Companies and research labs should communicate clearly about what their AI systems do, how they're tested, and how they collect or process data.
- **Shared Standards:** Global partnerships and standards can mitigate "AI arms races," ensuring mutual accountability and promoting beneficial applications.
- **Education for All:** Empower people at every educational level to understand AI fundamentals, so they can make informed decisions in their careers and civic life.

No matter how sophisticated AI agents become, the responsibility to guide them ethically—upholding human dignity, equality, and justice—remains in our hands.

12. Final Thoughts

From healthcare breakthroughs to personalized education and city-scale coordination, AI agents have already shown glimpses of their vast potential. In the coming years, their influence will likely extend even further, touching almost every sphere of life. Whether we're facing climate crises, seeking medical miracles, or trying to connect with others across cultural divides, AI's capacity to learn and adapt could be a pivotal ally—or a source of new hazards if we neglect responsible stewardship.

Through the chapters of this book, we've journeyed from the origins of AI and the technical underpinnings of intelligent agents to the nuanced challenges of ethics, regulation, and societal disruption. We've also explored practical strategies for organizations to adopt AI responsibly. This final look ahead underscores the magnitude of what's at stake: the shape of our future societies, economies, and personal freedoms.

The AI revolution isn't a spectator sport—it's a participatory enterprise requiring contributions from scientists, engineers, philosophers, lawmakers, and everyday citizens. By staying informed, challenging biases, insisting on transparency, and championing equitable solutions, we can guide AI agents toward a future that benefits us all. Instead of fearing machines that might overshadow humanity, we can harness their capabilities to amplify our collective intelligence, creativity, and compassion—writing the next chapter of human progress together.

www.ingramcontent.com/pod-product-compliance
Lightning Source LLC
LaVergne TN
LVHW010319220926
848484LV00004BB/792